Phil Moon's
Christian Survival Kit

MONARCH
Crowborough

Front cover and text illustrations by Taffy Davies

British Library Cataloguing-in-Publication Data.
A catalogue record for this book is available
from the British Library.

ISBN 1 85424 269 5

Designed and Produced in England for
MONARCH PUBLICATIONS
The Broadway, Crowborough, East Sussex TN6 1HQ by
Nuprint Ltd, Station Road, Harpenden, Herts AL5 4SE

Contents

For Christopher and
Katherine

Some of the inspiration for this book came from one of
the same title written by John Dixon and published by St
Matthias Press in Australia.

That's a really good book, but a bit too Australian
to be circulated over here, hence a slightly more
English version.

Please don't read this

Being a Christian is not a spiritual sega game

This book is for three people. Or more precisely for three sorts of people. Maybe you've just become a Christian. If so this book is for you. It will clarify what you've done, and talk about what happens next. Maybe you're just looking at Christianity. If so, this book is for you. It will show you what a Christian is, and what being a Christian is like. Maybe you've been a Christian for a while, but want some sort of refresher course. A spring clean, washdown and revitalisation. If so, this book is for you too. It will remind you of things you know about God, and hopefully encourage you to be more serious about him.

Christianity is a serious business. It's often brilliant fun, but it's not just a hobby or some sort of spare-time activity. It's not a religious rave or a spiritual SEGA game. It's more important than that. It's about who your friends are (and aren't), and the things that really matter to you. It's about the biggest decisions you ever have to make in life, and how you're going to cope with the next 60 years and more. And it's about where you spend eternity, and how useful your life is going to be, here on earth.

Christianity is a big business, and becoming a Christian is the biggest thing you could ever do. Mind you, not everyone becomes a Christian in a big blaze of glory. Take me, for instance...

I'm not sure when I became a Christian. I drifted into it from a completely non-Church background when I was 17 or 18. It all happened through a friend of mine at school who invited me along to his church youth group.

They were a pretty friendly bunch, and as I gradually became part of the group, their faith became mine.

And it's changed my life.

Now I think differently. I speak differently. I act differently. And I'm now working for an organisation which helps leaders of the sorts of groups through which I became a Christian.

So whether you're a Christian or not, this book is for you. I hope you enjoy it.

But more than that, I hope it might help to change your life—just a little bit. That's why, at the end of each chapter, there's a 'Digging in' section, which has a few ideas to help you begin to put into practice some of the things I've been talking about in that chapter. It will also have a few more Bible verses to look at, so that you can begin to think a bit more about these things as well.

Christianity is big. There's a huge amount to learn, and it will make a huge difference to your life. So why not begin as you mean to go on, taking it seriously.

2

Been there, done that

If a baby is born in a flower bed is it a flower?

This is a book about being a Christian. So it's a good idea, somewhere near the start, to work out just what exactly a Christian is. And isn't.

As part of my current job, I travel around the country, and tell young people about God, and about being a Christian. One of the things which always amazes me is that so many people have no idea what a Christian is.

Some people think you're a Christian if you're born in a Christian country. 'England is a Christian country' (yes, some people still believe that), 'so I must be a Christian'. Nonsense.

Anna is my wife. She's also a doctor, and in the past has played scrum half in a hospital baby delivery suite. One day they had an emergency call from the car park, where a lady hadn't quite made it in time, and had produced in the flower bed.

To say that being born in a Christian country makes you into a Christian is like saying that that baby must either be a car or a flower. Like I said: nonsense.

Some people are very nice. Perhaps you're one of them. But don't think that being nice makes you into a Christian. If that's the case, how come Jesus reserved some of his harshest criticism for those awfully nice Pharisee people? Again, more nonsense.

Others think that if your good deeds outweigh your bad, you'll get to Heaven, so you must therefore be a Christian. Yet more nonsense. What do you think God does? Sit there with a pair of celestial scales and a running total of your past deeds? If God is perfect, his standards must be the highest possible. Our problem is not so much one of our good outweighing our bad; our problem is that in order to be acceptable to God, we've got to behave to the highest possible standards, all the time. I haven't managed to do that yet, and even in my very best moments I hardly get within sniffing distance of God. And the Bible tells me that you don't fare much better.

So what *is* a Christian?

A Christian is a follower of Jesus Christ. That is, someone living with Jesus Christ as their Master, their King. Their Boss.

It's a relationship, a friendship. In order to see how that could begin, we need to go back a few steps.

Here is a simple outline to help you (and me) remember what God has done for us.

God

He created the universe and therefore this world, and you and me. If you make something, it bears your stamp, and you have authority over it. It's the same with God and us. We bear his stamp (his 'image', the Bible calls it), and he has the right to rule over us. That means that God has the right to tell you and me how to live our lives. But we don't like that idea much. That's exactly what the next point is about.

People

People don't like the thought of God ruling over us, so they rebel against it. They declare independence of God, saying in their hearts, 'Shove over God, I'm in charge here. You don't run my life, I do.' We all reject God by trying to run life our own way without him. The Bible calls that rebellion, sin.

I used to think 'Sin is nothing to do with me'. When I was 16, sin was just another religious word to be ignored.

Unfortunately you can't just ignore sin. You're intimately bound up with it. And sin screws you up.

Sin screws up your relationships. In a perfect world there would be no heartbreak, tears, anger, pride, selfishness, divorce, jealousy, resentment. In a perfect world there would be no bust up relationships. You'd get on with your parents. Other people wouldn't use you—in fact they would think you were really important, and they would respect you for who you are.

But the world isn't perfect. Sin exists, and it brings no end of pain and sadness.

And sin screws up our world. The Bible tells us that planet Earth is being slowly devastated by the results of our sin. Work has become toil, illness and suffering have arrived. The Earth lurches from disaster to disaster. The whole created world 'groans', because sin has put a large spanner in the works.

But most of all, sin screws up our relationship with God. It separates us from God. God is perfect, he won't have sin, or sinful people in his presence. Sin and God don't mix.

It's a little bit difficult to have a relationship with someone when the moment you're alone together you get burnt up. So, if we're going to have a relationship with God, the sin needs to be sorted out.

And that's just what God has done. We couldn't have done it (you can't pull yourself out of a pit), but thankfully, God has.

God

He loves you. He wants to be friends with you, to have a relationship with you. So he has sorted out our problem of sin.

God sent his son, Jesus Christ, to die for our sin. We deserve to die: he died in our place. He loved us so much that he was willing to die as our substitute, instead of us. Incredible.

Isn't it funny how sometimes events in the news can really stick in your mind? Over 10 years ago a plane crashed into a bridge in the middle of Washington D.C. and the wreckage fell into the icy Potomac river. I guess I remember it because the TV crews were quickly on the scene, and the rescue was seen live on TV.

Despite being right in the middle of Washington D.C., only five people were rescued. All five told the same story. They were in the icy water, and were handed a line from a helicopter by a man who had it first. When the helicopter came back a sixth time, the man had disappeared and drowned while saving the other five.

That man died so that they might live.

The incredible fact is that Jesus Christ died to save you and me—that *we* might live.

The punishment for our sin has been taken by Jesus, so he can offer us forgiveness. And because Jesus was raised to life again as the ruler of the world, he can offer us new life with God. That is the most amazing thing in the world. But this twin offer of forgiveness and life is not something he forces on us. Rather, he makes us an offer which we can accept or reject.

People

So it's up to you. You've got a choice. Accept the offer of life, have your sin forgiven, and live life God's way. Or reject it. Which may seem okay now, but means an eternity separated from God. Jesus called that, Hell.

God

In the end, God has the final word. He has appointed Jesus as judge of the world. Jesus will return to earth to wind it up, and he will take those who have accepted this offer of forgiveness and life, and are living God's way, to be with God for ever. Brilliant! But those who aren't Christians will be shut out. For ever.

That is what Christians call the Gospel.

Maybe you believe all that, have committed yourself to following Jesus Christ and are therefore a Christian. Great! But don't be smug about it. All you've done is accept a brilliant present.

Maybe you're thinking about it. Great, too. But don't spend so long thinking about it that you never actually do anything about it. You can spend so long looking at the times of last trains, that you miss the last one. Please don't do that. Read the rest of this book. Read other, better books. Talk to friends. Ask questions like 'Does Christianity hold water?', 'Is it true?', 'What must I do about it?' And then once you've made up your mind about being a Christian, don't dither. Actually do something about it, like, for instance, committing yourself to God.

Or maybe you are just like me. Between 15 and 18 I drifted into being a Christian. I gradually started believing what Christians believe, and behaving how Christians behave. I adopted their faith. And then I had a chat to our youth leader while we were away on a youth group holiday. And I look back to that time and say 'I *probably* was a Christian before then, but I *definitely* was from that time on.' That conversation clinched it for me. I've been a Christian since then.

If you're like me, you may find it helpful in the future to be able to look back and pinpoint a time when you committed yourself to God.

You could do it today, just quietly on your own. Simply tell God you believe all this God-People-God-People-God bit, and that you want to live life his way from now on and forever.

Then make a note of the date. You may find it handy in the years to come.

You could do that kind of thing at any time. If, while you're reading this book, you feel that you now understand enough about Christianity, and that you want to do something about it, simply tell God that you believe it, and that you want to live his way from now on.

And whenever you do that, make a point of telling someone within the next 24 hours. That may not be very easy, and you may find it embarrassing. But I'll guarantee that you'll find that first public profession of your new faith very helpful indeed.

DIGGING   IN

1. Get hold of a cheap notebook. Most of these 'Digging in' sections will suggest that you write something down.

2. Go through the God-People-God-People-God outline, and see how much you can remember. Ask a friend if you can try and explain it to them. Don't tell people 'It's all a case of "God-People-God-People-God".' Just have the outline in the back of your mind as a memory jogger.

3. Look up the following verses, which form the basis of the God-People-God-People-God outline. Match the verses to the particular part of the outline that they refer to:

   > Revelation 4:11;
   > Romans 3:10−12;
   > Hebrews 9:27;
   > 1 Peter 3:18;
   > 1 Peter 1:3;
   > John 3:36.

4. When learning the outline, you don't have to practise just on your Christian friends. Ask one or two of your non-Christian friends if they can help you.

5. If you're really keen, memorise the verses, and the outline, and pray for opportunities to try it out on non-Christian friends.

What's the difference?

...not necessarily a change you will notice straight away...

I f at all possible, this chapter will be even more riveting than the last. That's because it covers one of the most important things in human history, and it concerns you.

What I want to explain is the amazing things that God has done in you if you have responded to the Gospel and said yes to living for Jesus. So hang in there and give it a go. This chapter isn't long, but it's got vital stuff which you'll need to get hold of if the rest of the book, and the rest of your life, is going to make sense.

What I want to do is to sketch out what happens to you when you become a Christian. Many people feel no different at all when they have made that first step of committing their lives to Jesus, and worry that their prayer has not worked. In fact, a huge change has taken place, but it's not necessarily a change that you will notice straight away. Well, you may, but equally, you may not.

This change is not a physical one. My large nose didn't suddenly shrink when I became a Christian. No—the change in your life when you became a Christian is far more important than that.

So what's happened? What is the difference?

Forgiven

God has a bad memory. Well, in one sense, anyway!

We, on the other hand, can have very good memories.

If someone tries to go out with your girlfriend or boyfriend, you may forgive them, but you're unlikely to forget. When I was going out with Anna (who's now my wife), a very good friend of mine also tried to go out with her. That didn't last very long, and I forgave him. I was even his best man at his wedding. But I've never quite forgotten it!

But God is a better forgetter. When we ask God to forgive us, he does. And he does it very well—so well in fact, that he forgets that we even did it in the first place.

When we're forgiven by God and reunited with him, as far as God is concerned, it's just as if we had never done it in the first place. Just as if you had never lied, just as if you had never stolen. Just as if you were never lustful, never gossiped, never slept with them, never...

Just as if you were perfect, always.

That's God's forgiveness.

And that means that if you have asked God to forgive you for something that you have done in the past, there is no need to feel bad about it any longer. The slate has been wiped clean. You are no longer guilty.

Good one, God.

Born again

When someone becomes a Christian they are born again. Take a look at Jesus chatting to this character called Nicodemus in John, chapter 3, verses 1–7:

> Now there was a man of the Pharisees named Nicodemus, a member of the Jewish ruling council. He came to Jesus at night and said, 'Rabbi, we know you are a teacher who has come from God. For no-one could perform the miraculous signs you are doing if God were not with him.'
>
> In reply Jesus declared, 'I tell you the truth, no-one can see the kingdom of God unless he is born again.'
>
> 'How can a man be born when he is old?' Nicodemus asked. 'Surely he cannot enter a second time into his mother's womb to be born!'
>
> Jesus answered, 'I tell you the truth, no-one can enter the kingdom of God unless he is born of water and the Spirit. Flesh gives birth to flesh, but the Spirit gives birth to spirit. You should not be surprised at my saying, "You must be born again." '

Nicodemus hasn't a clue what Jesus is on about.

He just hasn't come across that kind of thing before. What Jesus is saying is that when you become a Christian you start from scratch, spiritually. A new person is born within you. Paul writes to the troublesome church at Corinth and says: 'If anyone is in Christ, he is a new creation' (2 Corinthians 5:17). So if you're 'in Christ' (that is, a Christian, a follower of God), you've started out afresh. You're a new person.

That's a fact. You may not feel it, like it, or look like it, but it's true.

We have some Australian friends. Some of them are native Australians, but we've also got one friend who went to live there, and ended up applying to become an Australian. She changed nationality.

The rules are complicated, but basically the idea is that if you live in a foreign country long enough, you can apply to become a citizen of that country. Now suppose you lived in Sydney for 10 years, and then decided you'd like to *be* an Australian.

You'd fill in various forms, wait for what seems like another 10 years and then the official documents come through. You are now an Australian. Do you look any different? No. Do you feel any different? Not much. But your status has changed overnight. You are now not an alien, but an Australian.

It's the same with God. When you become a Christian, your status with God changes. He now recognises you not as a foreigner, but as one of his, a Christian. You belong to him for ever.

Part of God's family

You're not only forgiven and born again, but when someone becomes a Christian they become part of God's family.

> For you did not receive a spirit that makes you a slave again to fear, but you received the Spirit of sonship. And by him we cry, 'Abba, Father.' The Spirit himself testifies with our spirit that we are God's children (Romans 8:15–16).

Not only do we belong to him, but he belongs to us. God becomes our 'Daddy' (that's what 'Abba' means in the above quote—it's not just the name of an ancient Swedish rock group). Jesus becomes our older brother, and all other Christians become your brothers and sisters.

You're related to them.

Some families on Earth aren't particularly brilliant, and if you belong to one of the less brilliant ones, I'm sorry. But everyone knows what a good family should be like. And God is our *good* father (or daddy), Jesus is our *good* older brother. The best older brother you could possibly hope for. And all other Christians may sometimes be a pain in the neck, embarrassing, awkward and completely fail to understand what you are on about, but despite that, you are related. You will spend eternity together in the biggest and best party ever. So hang in there with them. And even if they're not making a great go of being a good brother or sister to you, try to care for them like Jesus cares for you. You *are* part of God's family so get to know your new relatives and let them get to know you.

You might even be surprised at how wise and interesting older people can be.

You have a future

Being a Christian is about going to Heaven. Whenever I think about Heaven, I very quickly run out of brain space. What will it be like with all those people there? What will it be like to live for ever? What will God be like? When Jesus tried to explain what Heaven would be like, he most often said it would be like one great big fantastic party. The best party ever.

> Praise be to the God and Father of our Lord Jesus Christ! In his great mercy he has given us new birth into a living hope through the resurrection of Jesus Christ from the dead, and into an inheritance that can never perish, spoil or fade—kept in heaven for you... (1 Peter 1:3–4).

Don't let anyone fool you by saying that the party is *now*. We have the odd taster; otherwise we wouldn't know what we are looking forward to. But the *real* party is in Heaven, and as Christians we look forward to that. And the thought of that keeps us going in the tough times now.

But all the best parties involve preparation, and this one is no exception. God has done and is doing his part, but we've got to get ready for it as well. So how do we get ready for it?

Be what you are

This is how we get ready.

The Bible tells us to get ready for the brilliant party in Heaven by starting to behave now in the same way that we will behave when we are at the party.

It will be the best party ever. And when we arrive, we will be changed. The sin, the rebellion, will be completely removed from us, so that we can stand in the very presence of God and not be burnt up. And we get ready for the party by getting the sin out of our lives, now. If you're a Christian, God sees you without sin in your life, as perfect. So we need to aim to be what in God's eyes, we already are.

> You are forgiven, so act like it.
> You are born again, so act like it.
> You are part of God's family, so act like it.
> You are heading for Heaven, so act like it.

We're going to be looking at what this involves in the rest of the book.

DIGGING IN

1. Have a think about the things you've just read, and then pray, thanking God for what he's done in your life.

2. Get a pen and paper, and note down two or three areas that you need to work on in order to get ready for heaven. Then ask God to help you to become more like him in these areas of your life.

3. Check out:

   > Psalm 13:3–4;
   > Colossians 1:13–14;
   > Romans 8:23;
   > 1 Peter 2:9–10;
   > 1 Thessalonians 4:13–18.

4. Team up with a teenager who's a Christian, and go and talk to a Christian who's over 70. Perhaps ask your youth leader to introduce you. Ask the older person if you can do anything for them, and try to get an invite around for tea. Aim to get to know two older Christians a month—it'll do you, and them, a lot of good!

Get up and grow
— how not to be a spiritual midget

The best spiritual food is the Bible

Babies are meant to grow, and generally, they do. Sometimes, however, they don't. When our daughter Katherine turned up, she decided to spend a lot of time throwing up, and she not only failed to grow, she actually shrunk. The doctors were getting worried, and we were just a bit concerned ourselves.

Well that's all sorted out now and Katherine is fit and well. But it illustrates the point that babies are designed to grow. No one aged 15 still weighs 8lbs. When you became a Christian, you were born again, spiritually, and in the early days of your Christian life, you're a spiritual baby. Physical babies and spiritual babies have at least one thing in common—they are designed to grow.

Some people in Third World countries do grow, and then a combination of drought, famine, and civil war strikes and we get the all too familiar, appalling pictures on our TVs. Legs so thin you could put your fingers right round them. Ballooning stomachs. Eyes like tired ping-pong balls. And flies everywhere.

Some Christians are a bit like that. They start off well, and grow up a bit spiritually, and then, sadly, starve. But there's a difference between people who starve spiritually, and those who are starving in Third World countries. There they are often the victims of drought and war. They don't want to starve, but they do. Christians, however, can sometimes starve *themselves* to death by going on a spiritual hunger strike.

God intends you to grow, and to keep on growing towards Christian maturity. In his letter to the Christians in Colossae, Paul outlines his aim for them: 'We proclaim him, admonishing and teaching everyone with all wisdom, so that we may present everyone perfect in Christ' (Colossians 1:28). What Paul wants to do with the Colossian Christians is present them to Jesus when he returns or when the Christians die (whichever comes first) as mature Christians. Another version has it 'perfect in Christ'. What does this mean? It means being like Jesus. And that means learning about him and finding out how he wants you to live. It means doing what he says, and becoming more and more like Jesus.

Christians have to get up and grow.

Get up and grow

How? The main way of growing spiritually is by feeding spiritually.

We have a dog. He, like God, is very nice, but there I think the similarity ends. Bramley (our dog) eats dog food. But sometimes he likes to help himself to other tasty morsels. A little while ago now, he thought a chicken carcass would make a pleasant change, so he set to work. But unfortunately chicken bones can be very dangerous for dogs. They splinter and can rupture the dog's guts. If that happens it can be goodbye Bramley. Thankfully it didn't happen, and Bramley is keeping strictly to his diet of Pal and Winalot.

On the other side of the kitchen, Katherine, who is now seven months old, tucks into some hideous mixture of pulped this and that. I'm glad she likes it, because the mere sight of it sends me reaching for the sick bowl. I much prefer a good hot curry—the hotter the better.

Babies and dogs don't like curry. The point is that you've got to eat the appropriate food for yourself if you're going to grow.

That's what Peter says:

> Therefore, rid yourselves of all malice and all deceit,
> hypocrisy, envy, and slander of every kind. Like newborn
> babies, crave pure spiritual milk, so that by it you may
> grow up in your salvation, now that you have tasted that
> the Lord is good (1 Peter 2:1–3).

If you are a Christian, you're a spiritual being, and spiritual beings need spiritual food. The best spiritual food is the Bible. It's the *only* food which will give you proper spiritual nourishment. And that's essential if you're going to grow up as a Christian. Without the Bible, as a Christian you'll be stunted, and probably spiritually deformed.

There is more on the Bible in Chapter 5, which will help you see just why it is so important for the Christian.

Some people may say you just need to pray or you just need to go to church, or meet with Christian friends, or spend time worshipping God, and you'll be fine.

No you won't.

If you and I are going to be healthy Christians, we must read our Bibles.

'Where's the nearest restaurant please?'

'So if the Bible is that important, what can I do to feed on it, and what sort of places will give me a square meal?'

How do you feed on the Bible?

First, read it yourself. It's a very good idea to try and read a bit every day. Find a time and a place where you won't be disturbed. Use one of the modern translations of the Bible, so you won't get bogged down by all the 'Thees' and 'Thous', and use one of the many aids that are around to help Christians do this. Ask an older Christian to fill you in on what's around, and what they found most helpful. Chapter 5 deals with more of the practicalities about how to understand it when you read it on your own.

Once you've got into the habit of reading a little bit every day, you could try reading longer chunks. You can read the Bible as you would a novel. You could even aim to read it through—yes all of it! See 'Digging in' for further ideas about this.

But most of us also need to be fed the Bible by other people. That means that we need to go to a church and to a youth group where the Bible is taught. You could read other Christian books which will help you understand the Bible, and go on a Christian holiday where they teach you the Bible. Your youth group may well be affiliated to a national organisation which puts on these sorts of ventures. Go on one. You'll have a fantastic holiday, and it will do wonders for your Christian life. (Don't worry—

they don't spend all the time Bible bashing. There are plenty of other things going on as well.)

But what's it really like?

Let's be clear about it: being a Christian is not always easy or plain sailing. Being a Christian doesn't exempt you from the trials and troubles of this life. It helps you to face them, but you do still have to face them, just the same as everyone else.

And being a Christian brings with it a load more troubles. If you take Christianity seriously, you will lose some friends, and:

> 'In fact, everyone who wants to live a godly life in Christ Jesus will be persecuted' (2 Timothy 3:12).

That may not happen now, but the Bible is telling us that it *will* happen sometime.

And being a Christian means working hard for God, when others have their feet up. It means struggling to get the sin out of our lives, and being single-minded about this when other people want us to compromise.

It's not easy. But it is, without a shadow of doubt, worth it. It's worth it for the friends and the enjoyment and the fullness of life now. But above all it's worth it because we're on our way to Heaven.

DIGGING IN

1. Some Christians make it their aim to read through the whole Bible every year. You may like to do the same, but DON'T just start at the beginning with Genesis and attempt to read it through. You're bound to get bogged down and give up. There are plenty of plans around to help you do this in a sensible way, and even a Bible, called *The Bible in one Year* which sets it all out for you, day by day. Wonderful. Have a word with an older Christian about a plan that would suit you. But if you are going to do it, you'll have to be very disciplined, so why not ask a friend to do it as well—that will help you both to keep going.

2. Look up the following Bible verses, and see what they tell you about the Christian life.

    > 2 Timothy 3:15–17;
    > Psalm 119:9–16;
    > 2 Corinthians 12:10;
    > James 1:2–4.

3. Read Psalm 119 (yes, all of it!). This mentions the Bible in every verse. What does it have to teach us about the role of the Bible in the life of the Christian?

4. Think carefully about your life now, and write down the possible areas where Christianity is going to have to make a difference. File this safely away, and go into the rest of your Christian life with your eyes open to what it will entail for you.

5

The Word
— making sense of the Bible

Find a place where you can be undisturbed

When I first became a Christian, I was going along to a youth group, and week in week out the speakers were saying 'Christians should read their Bibles every day'. I didn't believe them. Surely no one in their right mind *ever* opens this black heirloom and reads it, let alone treats it seriously enough to take any notice of what they read?

How wrong can you be?

The youth group speakers kept up their barrage of 'Christians read the Bible every day', and in the end I thought I would give it a go. 'If you are going to be a Christian', this seventeen-year-old reasoned, 'you had better do what Christians do, and read the Bible. Daily.' And I did. And I thank God that I did, because it wasn't, and isn't, just a book. As I read it, I was being dealt with by God. And that is the way it works today.

Just what is the Bible?

The Bible is a fantastic book.

It is the Word of God, i.e. it is God communicating with human beings, at all times and in all countries, in ways that we can understand.

The Bible is God speaking. It is God telling human beings what he is like. It is God revealing Himself to us. The Bible is God's word, written. So as we read the Bible today, God speaks to us. It is in fact God's main way of communicating with the likes of you and me. The Bible is a very, very important book.

Now, of course, the Bible may be God's word, but he used people to write his words down. They weren't walking word processors though. What happened was that God used people who put themselves at his disposal, and the end result is literally 'God breathed'. We say the Bible is inspired. It is. But it is more accurate to say it is expired. By God.

So God breathed out his word through 40 or so different writers, and what we have now is 100 per cent human (the writers put their own stamp and personality on this), and also 100 per cent what God wants. It is God's Word. To us.

Well, that may be true, but the Bible can still be a pretty strange book...

Funny language

A lot of people think the Bible is full of funny language, littered not only with 'Thees' and 'Thous' but also little gems like 'behest', 'begat', and (best of all, I think) 'whist not'. That is in the old Authorised Version sometimes called the King James, because he was the man who authorised it. You will probably find it easier to read a more modern translation. And that's what the Bible is: a translation. It was originally written in Hebrew (most of the Old Testament), Greek (New Testament), with a little bit of Aramaic thrown in to confuse things!

So when you read any English version, it is a translation of the original languages. I like to use the New International Version (NIV) because it is up to date and an accurate translation. You may prefer the Good News Bible (GNB, although sometimes called TEV), which takes out some of the more complicated words, and is a freer translation. Have a look at the different ones and see which one you like.

When you look at a modern version, you'll see that it's not quite such funny language after all.

Funny style

The Bible has a number of different types of writing in it.

While I was going out with Anna, I went off to college and, as you do, we wrote to each other. While at college, I also had to write essays, fill in job applications, write prayer letters for the Christian Union, and so on. When I wrote to Anna, I didn't start 'In consideration of this subject it will be necessary to discuss the merits and demerits of the above statement'. Nor did I finish my letters 'Yours faithfully'.

There are different styles of writing, so we shouldn't be

surprised to find different bits of the Bible written in different ways. There are love songs, letters, history books, prophecies, and lots more. Bear that in mind when you are reading it, and don't expect it all to be in the style of 'Smash Hits'.

Funny layout

Open the Bible anywhere and you will see a forest of numbers. At first sight it looks confusing, but it is actually a very handy way of being able to find a particular bit of the Bible.

Each Bible book is divided up into chapters (unless it is very small, like 3 John), and each chapter is divided into verses. The larger numbers in your Bible are the chapter numbers, and the smaller numbers (usually right in there with the rest of the words), are the verse numbers. So John chapter 3 verse 16 means the sixteenth verse of the third chapter of John's gospel.

Then just to complicate things, the book title is often shortened, so John becomes Jn, Leviticus becomes Lev, Exodus becomes Ex, etc.

Sometimes there are two books of the same name. In this case we call them, for example, 1 and 2 Corinthians— i.e. the first and second letters Paul wrote to the church at Corinth. (Except here, to be absolutely truthful, Paul wrote three letters, but someone somewhere lost the second one, so to stop people looking for the second one which no longer exists, we have called the third one, 2 Corinthians. Got it?!)

Right, let's get back to the beginning. The Bible is God's Word. And it is written so that we can understand what God is like and what he wants us to do. It's brilliant stuff. It's just got to be read.

But how?

A time and a place

First, find a time and a place where you can be on your own and undisturbed. Tricky, huh? Well, think creatively.

It doesn't have to be at home. Try the bus or the train. Is there somewhere at school? Or a friend's house? Set aside some time. Try fifteen minutes, but don't worry if you struggle to fill it at first. If you are doing it at all, that's brilliant.

Get help

Help yourself by using a readable version, like the Good News Bible, or the New International Version, which I mentioned above.

Use something like Bible reading notes. Scripture Union produce ones like *Alive to God* and *Daily Bread*. There are other good things around, so ask your youth leader or an older Christian you know to help you on this.

And then ask for help from God. In other words, pray.

When you're at school, and struggling to understand *A Midsummer Night's Dream*, wouldn't it be a vast help if William Shakespeare could come and help you understand what he was on about? When you pray, you are actually asking God to do just that—you are asking the author to help you to understand what he has written. So every time you read the Bible, ask God to help you understand it. And ask him to help you put it into practice.

Use your brain

You are meant to use your brain when reading the Bible. That is not to say that it should become an academic exercise, but it should certainly be a thoughtful one.

Think about two things in particular:

1. Think about the context. Those nice people who wrote the Bible wrote their bit in a particular order, one sentence after another. So when you are trying to work out what it is about, look at the surrounding bits, and ask questions like 'Why does he say that here?' and 'How does this bit follow on from that bit?' Don't get all intel-

lectual about it, but do try to use your brain, just a little bit.

2. Think about history. Put yourself in their shoes. If you were a Jew in Jerusalem, at the receiving end of one of Jeremiah's prophecies, what impact would it have on you? If you were a Christian in Colossae, and had Paul's letter read to you, what difference would it make to you and the church?

You might need to find out a bit about the history of the Bible, so do ask an older Christian to help and perhaps ask for a good book like *The Bible From Scratch* (Simon Jenkins, Lion), for a Christmas present.

The Bible changes lives

The Bible is a practical book, so when you read it, see how you can apply it to your life. You won't be able to apply all of it, but a lot of it will be directly relevant to how you live your life. It may be 2000 and more years old, but it's as up to date as any book can be.

So when you're reading the Bible, look out for commands to obey, examples to follow (or bad examples to avoid!), and other less obvious applications. Ask God to help you see what relevance it has for you today. And then above all, once you know what God wants you to do, get on and do it.

That's not easy, so carry on praying that God will help you to do what he wants you to.

Write

Jot down what you have learned, and are going to do. It's well worth the effort. Get hold of a little notebook and start jotting.

If the Bible really is God speaking, then you will be dealt with by God when you read it. So it's worth writing down what's happening.

There was an Austrian concert pianist who used to claim that if he didn't practise for a day, he would notice the difference. If he didn't practise for a week his family would notice the difference, and if he didn't practise for a month his audiences would notice.

It's like that with reading the Bible: it actually makes a big difference to your life. If you don't read it, you'll notice, then your friends and family will notice and then complete strangers will begin to notice.

But if you were to go away and read your Bible every day for a year, put it into practice and then come back in a year's time, I guarantee that you would be a transformed person.

It's that kind of book.

DIGGING IN

1. Look up these verses and see what they have to say about the nature of the Bible:

   Psalm 19:7−14;
   2 Timothy 3:14−17.

2. Ask for *The Bible from Scratch* for Christmas.

3. If there is a 'Walk Thru' the Bible' in your area, go. And take your friends. If there isn't one, see if you can get your church to organise one.

4. Make an agreement with a friend that you will try to read your Bible every day, using the same Bible reading notes. If you don't understand something, ask them about it. If they don't understand it either, ask someone else in your church. If you read something that's incredible, tell your friend about it. That should help you to keep going on it when you would rather be doing something else!

Inside story — the who, what and why of the Holy Spirit

The Holy Spirit is a trainer

guess you've heard of the Holy Spirit. Perhaps you get along to church and they say the creed, including the line 'I believe in the Holy Spirit'. Perhaps you've heard people pray, asking God to do something 'through your Spirit'.

But who is the Holy Spirit? What does the Holy Spirit do? And why do Christians think the Holy Spirit is so important?

These are big questions. And they can get quite complex. This short chapter can't give you all the answers. But it will, hopefully, point you in the right direction.

Who is the Holy Spirit?

Note that I said 'who' and not 'what'. The Holy Spirit is a *person*—not an object or a thing. He is an individual.

But the big answer to the question 'Who is the Holy Spirit?' is to say that he is God. 100 per cent God. You've got all of God that there is, in the Holy Spirit. But this all begins to get incredibly complex. Because the Bible also tells us that God the Father is God, and that Jesus the Son is God as well. Three persons, all 100 per cent God, who together form one God. That's what Christians call the Trinity.

I was never very good at maths at school, but even I know that 1+1+1 does not equal 1. But that's what the Bible tells us: God is One, and God is also Three. All very complicated, and in the end impossible to understand. But don't let that put you off. Wouldn't you expect God to be impossible to understand fully?

So the Holy Spirit is 100 per cent God, a person, and part of the Christian Trinity, which states that God is one in three persons: Father, Son, and Holy Spirit.

The Holy Spirit is an important person. And a busy one. These are some of the major projects he's involved with...

What does the Holy Spirit do?

A fair question. One of the most important things the Holy Spirit does is to come and live in people who follow Jesus.

If you're a Christian, you have the Holy Spirit.

When you make a Christian commitment, putting God first, and beginning to live your life for him, you are given the Holy Spirit. Some gift!

Now that's got certain advantages. Here are a few...

The Holy Spirit is a helper

The Holy Spirit helps us live like Jesus.

When I was 12 I wanted to be a racing driver.

Driving a car around a race track, breaking the lap record, and staying alive, is a pretty tricky thing. I could manage two of those, but probably not the third. But suppose I invited Nigel Mansell or Damon Hill to take my place. Now that's a different story...

Jesus may not be too bothered about driving racing cars, but he is bothered about helping us live our lives the way he wants us to. And when the Holy Spirit comes into our lives, he helps us to do just that.

The Bible uses a number of words to describe the Holy Spirit. One is 'comforter'. Strange word, comforter. And old fashioned too. In fact it's used in the Bayeux tapestry, where King William is shoving a spear into the backside of one of his troops, and the caption reads 'William comforteth one of his men'. 'Comforter' in the Bayeux tapestry, and in the Bible, means to spur into action. That's what the Holy Spirit does, for you, and me.

We still have to do the action. But the Holy Spirit helps us, gives us the ability, if you like, to change, and become more like Jesus in the way we live our lives.

And as we work with the help of Spirit, to live like Jesus, he produces fruit in our lives. The fruit of the Spirit is love, joy, peace, patience, kindness, goodness, faithfulness, gentleness and self-control. You might be surprised to find these growing in your life as you seek to live like Jesus. You may not notice them at first. But others will.

The Holy Spirit is an enabler

The Holy Spirit equips God's people to do God's work.

Have you ever tried to play hockey without a stick? Or paint without a brush? Or pick your nose without a finger? Tricky, huh?

As God's people, he gives us jobs to do, and also gives us gifts to get the jobs done. Spiritual gifts, they're called, and God gives us these to equip us to serve him.

These gifts include things like the gift of being an evangelist or a pastor/teacher, gifts like speaking in tongues (or different languages), prophecy, administration and so on. There are lots and lots of gifts (more than the lists mentioned in the Bible in 1 Corinthians 12, Romans 12 and Ephesians 4).

This is an area where Christians have different opinions. To be honest we don't even know what all the gifts were that the early church had. And to be even more honest, who cares? What the Bible says is that we should use these gifts that we have, to benefit his church (i.e. other Christians), and to glorify God.

The church at Corinth seemed to be good at speaking in tongues, prophecy, and things like that. Okay, fine. What Paul says is 'Use these to benefit the church and glorify God'. You may have other gifts. That's fine too—just make sure you use them to benefit the church and glorify God.

Remember therefore, that all your gifts should be used to build up the people of God, so that God is glorified.

The Holy Spirit is a communicator

One of the Holy Spirit's jobs is to communicate with human beings about God.

He does this in a number of ways. Take, for example, what Jesus said in John 16:8:

> When he (i.e. the Spirit) comes, he will convict the world
> of guilt in regard to sin, and righteousness and judgment.

In other words the Spirit will convict you, me and our
friends of our need for God. That's important stuff. We
can't do it—we need the Spirit to work in our friends'
lives to convince them that they need God.

One of the most important ways that the Holy Spirit
communicates is linked in closely with the Bible. They go
together, like bread and butter, Guns 'n Roses, orange
juice and muesli. (Well, I like orange juice on my muesli
anyway!)

Take, for example, John 14:26:

> But the Counsellor, the Holy Spirit, whom the Father
> will send in my name, will teach you all things, and will
> remind you of everything I have said to you.

Here Jesus tells the twelve disciples that the Spirit will
help them remember what he's been saying. He's com-
missioning them to write down the New Testament, with
the help of the Holy Spirit.

(In Chapter 5 we saw that the Bible is inspired by the
Holy Spirit of God, working through the writers.)

And then, having been involved in the writing, the
Holy Spirit helps us to understand the Bible. Paul writing
to his friend Timothy, tells him:

> Reflect on what I am saying, for the Lord will give you
> insight into all this (2 Timothy 2:7).

Paul is saying that Timothy has to use his brain to understand what he (Paul) is writing, and also rely on the Spirit.
The Spirit helps you and me to understand God's word as
we engage our brains to understand it. So ask him to help
you each time you read it.

The Holy Spirit also helps us to communicate with
God:

> In the same way, the Spirit helps us in our weakness. We do not know what we ought to pray for, but the Spirit himself intercedes for us with groans that words cannot express (Romans 8:26).

Some groaning! We're not very good at communicating with God. That's the news from Romans 8:26. So the Holy Spirit helps us pray, as he prays for us. When it comes to praying, I need all the help I can get, and thankfully the Spirit is right there where it counts.

Those are some of the major things the Holy Spirit wants to be up to in your life. There are others too, of course, but I don't want to go on for ever about him, not just at the moment anyway.

What's my job?

I guess it would be easy to just lay back, relax, take it easy, and let the Holy Spirit get on with the job of winging you to Heaven. Take a holiday. Don't do anything. 'Let go and let God.'

Unfortunately, that is complete rubbish. And dangerous rubbish at that.

I like sport. Never was particularly good at it, but I love playing hockey, squash, tennis, and I even rowed, once upon a time.

If you are going to be really good at sport, you could have a sauna, jacuzzi, and massage, but I don't think it would do a lot of good. No, you've got to get into shape. And you've got to practise.

Being a Christian is not about attending some cosmic massage parlour where you lie back and get knocked into shape. We are talking more about a gym. The Holy Spirit is a trainer, not a masseur. He's there to help us, push us, and encourage us to be more like Jesus. To do that, he helps us understand the Bible and therefore see what Jesus is like, and how we can live lives that please him. And he 'comforts' us, to keep us hanging in there, and become a little more like Jesus each day.

DIGGING IN

1. Ask for a concordance for Christmas or your birthday. A concordance is a bit like a dictionary, and it helps you find particular words in the Bible. Get a concordance which is matched up to your version of the Bible, and look up at least some of the references to 'Holy Spirit' and 'Spirit'. This may take a little while, so set aside some time to do this. Note down what you find out, under separate headings, like those in this chapter.

2. Pray about what you have found out. Thank God for the Holy Spirit, and ask him to help you co-operate with the Holy Spirit as he sets to work in your life to make you more like Jesus.

3. Work out what gifts the Holy Spirit has given you. Ask others who know you what they think. Then begin to work out ways that you can develop and use these gifts to serve other Christians and to glorify God.

7

·················

Talking to yourself or changing eternity? Getting praying

The Vidal Sassoon position

Praying—it's something religious people do. It's something most people do when they're in trouble. It's something weird. It's something surrounded by misunderstanding.

Prayer is an extraordinary thing. Think for a moment about what God is trying to do: the Creator of the universe is taking the trouble to involve you in what he is up to on planet Earth. He wants to line up your life with his and he wants you to be part of his plans for the future of mankind. He actually wants you to talk to him. He wants you to tell him how you're feeling and what your hopes and fears are. He wants to build a relationship with you. And all good relationships have good communication.

Prayer is communicating with God.

Now that really is weird. And yet we still neglect it. That's just perverse. How can you possibly neglect something quite so amazing and fundamental as this?

I was told once that prayer is spiritual breathing: vital for life so don't stop doing it. That's just about it. This is a vital thing for every Christian. And it's something you can do on your own or with other people.

On your own

'OK, sounds like a good idea, I'm going to pray. How?'

First, set aside some time each day. It would be dumb for me to say 'You must pray for 10 minutes each day'. I don't build my marriage by saying 'Right Anna, I'm going to talk to you for 10 minutes each day—from 9:49 to 9:59 each evening'. That's not the way relationships work (at least not mine). So don't treat God like that either.

But praying is one of those things that gets left out if you don't work at it, so it's a great help to find a bit of time that you can set aside for this purpose.

Find somewhere quiet where you won't be interrupted. Or go for a walk (take the dog with you). So make sure you have a special time set aside for God, each day. And then guard it! There will be all sorts of pressures on you to use this time for other things. Learn to say 'No' to these other things, because this time with God must be a priority.

Try and pray at other times as well, just as you go through the day. Talk to God when you wake up, and just before you go to sleep. Let the things and people you see and think about become the things and people you pray for. Also, pray for the things and people you see in the news, for your church, for next Sunday's services, for your local community, your local schools and doctors... the list is endless.

I've been struck loads of times by Samuel's farewell speech to the people of Israel, in which he says:

> As for me, far be it from me that I should sin against the Lord by failing to pray for you (1 Samuel 12:23).

To pray for others is, simply, just part of our Christian duty.

I hope all that will help you pray for other people. You can also pray for yourself. And for all the things that you are doing and involved with. Remember too, that praising and thanking God are important things to do. It's a natural thing to praise good and wonderful things and people. Presumably you rave about your favourite group or film star. Do it with God too. And thank him, for all he's given you, and for all he's done for you—he deserves it.

Changing the subject slightly, I do things which get up God's nose. I do things that make God angry; things which spoil our relationship. I sin. So do you. One of the things we need to do when we pray is to say sorry to God. The posh word for this is confession. So make a habit of saying sorry, and therefore putting things right between you and God. The Bible tells us: 'If we confess our sins, he is faithful and just and will forgive us our sins and purify us from all unrighteousness' (1 John 1:9). So don't get paranoid about sin, but do be realistic about it, say sorry, and with God's help try to do better next time out.

Praying with others

People really get worried about prayer meetings. They get paranoid, tongue-tied, and petrified at the thought of praying out loud, and then botching it up.

I remember the first prayer meeting I ever went to. One of my friends conned me into going by saying there would be coffee at someone's home afterwards, and (the liar) he even claimed that this meeting would be fun. You cannot be serious.

I spent about the most awkward 46 minutes of my life as we broke into little groups, got into the Vidal Sassoon position (i.e. crouch forward as if about to wash your hair in a sink), and then using special language, spoke to someone who, as far as this sixteen-year-old was concerned, may not even have been there. I don't think I made it to another prayer meeting for another eight or nine months, by which time at least I recognised that there was someone there listening.

If you think about it though, if two Christians are together it's a natural thing to want to talk to the invisible but real third person who's there with them. It's called a prayer meeting, and prayer meetings are rather special things.

> Again I tell you, that if two of you on earth agree about
> anything you ask for, it will be done for you by my
> Father in heaven. For where two or three come together
> in my name, there am I with them (Matthew 18:19–20).

It's a great privilege to be able to talk to God with your friends. But a lot of people get very uptight about it. Talking to God with your friends just isn't something to get worried about. Forget the flowery language, be yourself, and relax.

You don't have to use all sorts of religious jargon or special formulas. Be normal, and chat to God together. Have a conversation with God. You don't have to say 'Amen' at the end and you don't have to conjure up an 'In your name' or 'For Jesus' sake' to let the others know you're coming to the end. Just chat to God, together. And if you start to pray out loud at the same time as someone else, it really doesn't matter. So don't get uptight about it. Have a laugh about it, say 'After you', and then get on with the business.

Just do it

Prayer is one of those things where it's terribly easy to do a lot of talking about it, but never actually get down and do anything about it. So we read a lot about prayer, we talk a lot about prayer, but we never actually pray.

So can I suggest that once you've looked at the 'Digging in' section, you spend just a little time, praying?

DIGGING IN

1. Please do what I've just suggested, and have a pray. Now?

2. Try making a prayer diary. Get a bit of paper and a pencil, and note down people and things you want to pray for every day. This could include, for instance, your parents and your church. Then write out the days of the week, and decide who and what you are going to pray for on each day. You can easily pray for people on two or three days a week—just write their names down more than once.

   Write in pencil, so that you can change it when you want to add new people to your prayer diary, or take some people and things off it.

   Now store it somewhere safe, like your Bible or diary, and aim to use it, every day.

   Don't be bound by a prayer diary. It should stimulate you to pray (perhaps especially when you don't really want to), and help you to remember the things and people you should be praying for. But don't be a slave to it.

3. Encourage prayer in your youth group. Ask your leaders to make sure that you pray together in every group meeting. Ask them if you can use one meeting every so often just to pray. Start up a group prayer news sheet. Ask other people what the group can pray for, and produce a monthly prayer sheet of things and people to pray for.

4. Get together with one or two friends once a week for ten minutes, and pray together. You could of course make it longer if you want!

5. Get hold of today's newspaper, go up to your bedroom, and pray for the people who are in the news, and for the situations that you read about.

A seriously boring place full of
seriously boring people?
What the Church is really like

It's worth getting to know the Sybils in your church

Let's be honest about it, church is a weird place. Where else (where people aren't drunk) do they sing together? Where else do they close their eyes and speak to someone who isn't there? Where else do they sit in rows on hard seats with funny names, and sit contentedly while some individual in a long white nightie drones at them from inside a wooden box (no, not a coffin) with a manner that is a certain cure for insomnia?

And yet going to church is still a popular activity in this country.

Why is that? To answer that, we need to ask what the church is, and what it isn't.

What *isn't* the church?

The church is not a building. We say 'I'm going to church', or 'Isn't that a beautiful church?'. That's talking about the church building. But when the Bible talks about the church it's not talking about a building. They didn't have church buildings then. Biblical churches are not bricks and mortar. That's not what the word means.

When you hear about the church on the news, they usually mean the dear old C of E—i.e. one particular denomination, or group of like-minded churches. The Bible has something to say about that, but that's not what it normally means by 'Church'.

What *is* the Church?

In the Bible 'church' is always a bunch of people. Christian people, who get together regularly to learn more about God, to talk to him and worship him, and to support and help each other in the Christian life. These days we tend to meet in buildings called churches, specially set aside for that purpose. But we don't have to. So always take care not to confuse the building with what the church really is—the people of God.

Why bother?

Bother because church is a group to learn from
When I was learning to drive, the car had two L plates. Then I passed my test, and my dad insisted that I carry on using L plates for a while, whenever I was driving his car. Sensible man, my dad, although I didn't quite appreciate it at the time. When you're driving, you take care of cars with L plates, make allowances, and steer well clear of them. So wearing L plates gives you more of a chance to learn, even if you *have* passed your test!

Christians wear L plates all through their lives. We are learners (that's what 'disciple' means). And church is a great group of people to learn from. Learn from the teaching on Sundays and mid-week, learn from each other and encourage one another to put into practice what you are learning. Whenever you go along to church, go along, among other things, to learn.

Bother because church is a group to belong to
I guess your home may not be a happy one. But don't let that hide the fact that the church is now your new spiritual home. It's a family, and it's a good one. It's where you belong, and probably where your best friends will be. So get stuck into your local church, because it will really help you in your Christian life. It will give you friends, support and encouragement. Just what the doctor ordered.

Bother because church is a group to give to
Church is a group to receive from. The Bible also tells us that church is a group to give to. If it's all get, get, get, someone is doing a lot of giving and you are doing all the taking. But church should be give and take. You *give* and you *take*. So think of your church and work out what you can give to them: give your time, your talents, give your energies and enthusiasm, and give your money. More of this, later!

Bother because of Sybil

So, church is worth bothering with. Now let's get in beyond the heavy oak door and take a closer look. But don't let me give the impression that church is just about what happens inside the church building on a Sunday. Well it is... but there's a lot more to it than that.

It's right that Christians should meet together regularly, but there's much more to it than just Sunday services. The Bible talks about the church as a body, as a living organism. We get together because we *are* together. We are part of each other. We belong to each other.

If you're a Christian, you have more in common with the Christian old dear called Sybil in the row in front than you have with any of your closest, non-Christian friends. That's because you and Sybil are both on your way to Heaven. You'll spend eternity together. (And she'll look an awful lot better in Heaven, too.)

So it's worth getting to know the Sybils in your church. There was a Sybil in a church I used to go to. She was a real star. Whenever you talked to her, you were uplifted and encouraged. She was really nice; she loved people and cared for them. She was holy (and some of it rubbed off), and she prayed for you.

Good old Sybil.

So get to know the Sybils in your church. Spend a bit of time with them. They're worth their weight in gold.

And, of course, if church is going to be a family, and not just a weekly meeting, you're going to have to spend a bit of time with all sorts of older and younger people in your church. That means doing things in and for your church, but not just on Sunday. If there are church social events, get a few of your Christian friends, and be there. Talk to other people, let them get to know you. Get stuck in.

That may not be very easy, of course. Most churches have a Sybil or two. Or more. For some though, there's not a Sybil in sight. Some churches don't appreciate young people. Your clothes are outrageous, your music is too loud, your haircut a disgrace. And as far as the earrings are concerned...

So there may be a few problems, but hang in there. They may be old fashioned, but there will almost certainly be Christians there. Love them, talk to them, be committed to them, and gradually get used to the idea of spending an eternity with each other.

What makes a good church?

It could be that you're interested in Christianity, or have become a Christian but haven't found a church to go to.

The trouble is, there are so many different churches—Methodist, Baptist, Brethren, House Church, Independent, Assemblies of God, C of E, URC and all sorts of other abbreviations you've never heard of. And different churches do things in different ways. How do I choose? What makes a good church?

Here are some guidelines. A good church is one where...

1.   The Bible is taught

As a Christian you need to learn from the Bible. So go to a church where you'll be taught it. This will teach you about God and therefore help you to get to know him better and love him more.

Being taught the Bible is also the Biblical way of making sure you remain on the rails, and don't drift off into the land of weird and loony religious ideas.

2.   Make it local

Try your *local* church. In the Bible, churches were all local—probably because people couldn't commute as they had no cars, trains, etc. But it's a good principle: go to a church near you.

I live in a village, and we chose to live there because it has a good church. In fact the village only has one church, and there's a lovely notice in the Adventurers room (i.e. Sunday School), made by one of the children, saying

'God's people in Bishop's Itchington'. I like that. That's what a local church should be.

3. Good leaders
You won't have a good church without good leaders. So do you like them? Can they teach you? Ask the minister what he wants to do with the church. What are his (her?) aims? What are their priorities and the methods they are going to employ?

4. Telling others
Is this church keen to tell their friends and people in the area about the gospel of Jesus? A good church is an outward looking one that sees the importance of telling people the good news about Jesus Christ.

5. Love for each other
Is your church growing in their care, love and concern for each other? You can probably see this the moment you walk in. Take a note too, of when they see each other during the week. You can't really love others when you sit in the row behind them for one hour, once a week, exchange pleasantries, and then go your own way, only to meet up again for more pleasantries next week.

Hanging in there
If you're a Christian, church is not an optional extra, like central locking, metallic paint or ABS. It comes as standard, and always has done.

You can't survive as a Christian and forget about church. It may not be easy. You may have to take the initiative. But Christians need each other to survive.

So hang on in there.

DIGGING IN

1. The first thing to do, if you don't do so already, is to start going to church—your local one if at all possible.

2. Read 1 Corinthians 12—14, and make some notes about what it tells you about what the church is like, and how the church should be run.

3. Read Ephesians—yes, all of it! It won't take you very long at all. As you read it, ask yourself the question, 'What has God got to do with the Church?'

4. With a friend, go and get to know some Sybils in your church.

Being a signpost
— but which way are you pointing?

Evangelism is like going fishing

You're at school.

Your youth leader has been telling the group it's vital for Christians to tell their friends about Jesus. Even the thought of it ties your guts in knots, but you've told your friends back home that you're going to give it a go. So as the bell goes for morning break you pile out of the classroom with everyone else, and then, palms sweating, announce with a slight tremble 'Can I tell you about Jesus?'

All talking comes to a crashing, grinding halt. They stop and stare at you. Your best friend says 'You trying to convert us?' 'No' you reply, weakly, 'not really'. And you walk away and resolve never to try that one again.

Sounds familiar? A familiar nightmare, or perhaps you've actually tried it.

When it comes to telling others about what we believe, it's very easy to go to extremes, adopting completely bizarre methods, or becoming totally mute. Here are some of the more exotic methods:

1. **RSPCA approach**
   You can go RSPCA, and adopt the line that evangelism (as it's called) isn't something you'd do to your dog, let alone your friends. So you leave well alone.

2. **Equity card approach**
   Every time you talk to your friends you get all dramatic, put on a performance and become someone you're not. Really helpful . . .

3. **The City Technology College approach**
   Which says that you've got to be trained before you can do anything. You must go on a course in personal evangelism before you ever say anything to anyone.

4. Hole in the ground approach

Which says that if I talk to my friends about Jesus, I'll stand out like a sore thumb, they'll laugh at me, it will be hideously embarrassing, and I'll wish a large hole in the ground would open and swallow me up. So I won't bother. Friends are much more important than being a witness.

I've used all those approaches from time to time. I'm quite good at some of them. It's far better though, to have:

5. A normal approach

The amazing thing about the normal approach is that we all do it, all the time!

Ever been a witness to a car crash? Or a crime? Or some other important event? Well you know what it's like—you arrive home breathless to tell the family what happened, and spend the next fortnight telling your friends every last detail. If you're lucky the police turn up and you have to give a statement. If you're extra lucky, you get called into court to give evidence as a key witness.

Now the amazing thing is that if you're a Christian, in just the same way, you are a personal witness to the most important event in the history of the universe. You have personally encountered the living God and have entered into friendship with him through Jesus.

You are a witness to the Gospel of Jesus Christ (for an outline of that, see Chapter 2). You might deny it in front of your friends (in which case you'd be a bad witness), or you can tell people the facts (in which case you'd be a good witness). Either way, there's no escaping the fact that you are a witness of some sort. The question is, are you a good witness, or a bad one? Good witnesses give an accurate account of what happened. Bad witnesses keep their mouths shut.

This chapter is about being slightly better witnesses.

Why bother?

But why should we bother to be slightly better witnesses? After all, it's far easier to keep your mouth shut.

We bother because God bothered. He sent his son to die for us, so that we might be forgiven.

A young English businessman was going home from work late on the train one evening, and shared his part of the train with two other men. As the train pulled out of the station, one of these two men started having a violent fit. The other one did what he could to help and once the fit was over, and the man recovering, his helper turned to apologise to the English businessman, and said in an American accent 'Look I'm very sorry, but you see this sort of thing happens often. We were in Korea together, in the war, and I was wounded out in no man's land. This Englishman came out to get me, and then just as we were almost back to safety another shell landed nearby. I woke up in hospital, got better, and left the army at the end of the war. Then I heard that this Englishman would never quite recover.

'So I resigned my job, broke off my engagement, sold my house and car, and came over here to look after him.

'You see he did that for me. There's nothing I wouldn't do for him.'

Jesus Christ was bothered enough to die for you and me. Surely we can be bothered enough just to tell our friends what he's done.

You are a witness. So am I. So let's aim to be slightly better ones.

How to be a slightly better witness

Here are 3 things to think about:

1.   Know it

If you're going to talk to someone, it helps if you know what you're going to say. That gives you confidence. So how about mugging up on:

Your story: How *did* you become a Christian? What were you like before? What happened when you became a Christian, and what's the difference now? Jot it down, and tell a Christian friend (without the notes!). Or, even better, tell a non-Christian friend.

The Gospel: Get the stuff from Chapter 2, and learn it, so if someone asks you what a Christian believes, you can tell them. Don't say 'Well it's God/people/God/people/God'. Just have that in your mind as you tell them.

Reasons: Begin to find out *reasons* why you believe what you believe. Ask people, read a book about it. Find out the questions people who aren't Christians are asking. Begin to find out how to answer things like 'You believe what you want to believe, and I'll believe what I want to believe, OK?' and 'How can God love the world with all this suffering around the place?'

Remember one thing when mugging up on things like this. There's no shame in saying 'I don't know.' Anyone with half a brain cell can recognise when you are struggling to explain something. What's important is your faith, not your knowledge.

2. Live it

For a start, just be yourself. Be natural and relaxed about it.

It's important to let them know you're a Christian on your first day in a new place. A friend of mine called Smeee (silly name, good friend), worked for Butlins as a Redcoat one summer.

It's very easy for the elastic in the moral underpants of a Butlins Redcoat to snap. So Smeee told them on the first day that he was there, that he was a Christian. They respected him for that, and so it was a lot easier for him to live a Christian life and talk to them about Jesus, because he had done that.

So let them know that you're a Christian.

Then do your best to live a Christian life—try to put into practice the stuff from the rest of this book.

They'll notice if you're different. If you don't get drunk and swear and sleep around like they do, they'll notice. You don't have to be freakish about it. Be normal.

Live it. They'll notice. The friend through whom I became a Christian spoke in public lots and lots about Christianity. I'm sure his talks were very good, but I can't remember a thing he said. What I *do* remember, and what made most impact on me was the way he behaved. Here was someone who took me seriously, and who cared about me. Here was someone who took the Bible seriously, and really tried to do what it said. This man was powerful stuff.

3. Tell it
But before you do, pray.

When I was at college a friend of mine prayed every day for one particular friend of his. As Tom grew warmer to Christianity, Nick began praying that Tom would become a Christian. Guess what? He did.

Pray for your friends. One will do. Be realistic what you pray about. So don't just pray that your utterly pagan friends will become Christians tomorrow. Pray first that they will be less aggressive to Christianity. Then start praying that they will show an interest and want to understand more about Christianity. And as they grow warm as Tom did, then you can start to pray that they will actually make a commitment.

4. Pray and look out
We've got to be really serious about praying for our friends. It's *the* big thing. We can't just leave the praying to others. Get together with your friends, in twos and threes, and pray (even very briefly) for your non-Christian friends. Pray for them on your own. Make a habit of it,

and as you pray, pray for opportunities to talk about Jesus.

I think it's true to say that whenever I've asked God at the start of a day for opportunities to talk to someone about him, he's always given me those opportunities.

So pray for, and look out for, opportunities to talk to your friends about Jesus. You don't have to be an expert to do it. You don't have to know all the answers. You just have to know Jesus, and be concerned that your friends don't.

5. God talk

Try too, bringing God into an ordinary conversation. Try things like 'I wonder what God thinks about that' or 'I shouldn't think God's terribly impressed' or 'That must make God very angry'. It's like going fishing. Lob some things into the general chit-chat and see if anyone's interested. If they start biting, someone's probably been praying, so don't stop now!

Talking to people about Jesus can be great fun. I'm not terribly good at it, and don't do it enough. But I love it. It's exciting and gives me a real buzz. I guess the fact of the matter is that the more you do it, the more confidence you have to do it. So go on, give it a go.

The very first Christians had no training courses, no methods of evangelism, no books. They just went out and told their friends. And no one could stop them. They were so caught up by the good news about Jesus, they just had to tell their friends.

So, get to know the Gospel. Read it again and again, and let it become part of you. Then pray, and be patient for God to do his work.

Then hang on in there.

DIGGING IN

1. Look up these verses, and see what they have to tell us about evangelism:

   > Matthew 28:19–20;
   > Acts 1:8;
   > Acts 2:47;
   > Colossians 4:2–6.

2. The Gospel itself is the greatest incentive for our evangelism. When we understand it more deeply, we will be more inclined to tell others about what we believe. So why not take out a couple of hours, and aim to read through the whole of Mark's Gospel? It won't take you as long as that, and it will help you understand the Gospel, and therefore be more enthusiastic about telling others.

3. Start praying every day for one or two of your non-Christian friends.

4. Get together with one or two of your Christian friends, and together pray for your non-Christian friends.

5. Pray for opportunities to talk to your friends about Jesus. Try to bring God into the conversation, and see if any of them 'bite'.

6. Get hold of a couple of Christian biographies or short books, that explain who Jesus was, what he did, or how people met him. Read them, and then lend them to your friends. 'I've just read this really good book...'

10
. . . .
His infernal majesty — the Devil is alive and kicking

*The Devil can suggest that you do things,
but he can't force you*

You are probably interested in the Devil. The Devil is, I'm afraid, a very interesting subject for many.

You find films and TV programmes, newspaper articles, books, magazines, songs, T-shirts, posters, graffiti in loos (well men's loos anyway, I'm not so sure about girls'). All on the subject of the devil.

If you're at a party and start talking with obvious authority about renaissance art, people will soon drift off to top up their already full glass. But if you're talking about the Devil, it's rapt attention. Why?

The Bible tells us that the Devil is one of the two main forces in the universe. You either serve God or the Devil. And human beings naturally want to know more about this whole spiritual area of life.

Where did the Devil come from?

Don't know. Well, at least, we can't be too specific. In the Old Testament there's a suggestion that the Devil is a fallen angel:

> How you have fallen from heaven O morning star, son of the dawn! You have been cast down to the earth, you who once laid low the nations! You said in your heart, 'I will ascend to heaven; I will raise my throne above the stars of God'...But you are brought down to the grave, to the depths of the pit (Isaiah 14:12–15).

It seems that the Devil is one of God's secret agents, gone bad. Very bad.

But we're not told very much about all this, so it's probably best not to speculate. The Bible tells us lots of other stuff, so let's find out what God *does* tell us about the Devil, rather than guess about what he *doesn't* tell us.

Why the Devil is interested in you

When you became a Christian you changed sides. You were on the Devil's side. Now you're on God's side. The Devil is now your enemy.

I also have a suspicion that the Devil is particularly interested in *you*. Do you ever go to a 'pick your own farm'? If you're picking raspberries, don't you go for the easy ones first? If you were a raspberry (just supposing...) you'd be one of those on the edge of the bush. You're new to Christianity, or you want a refresher course. As far as the Devil's concerned, you're probably fairly easy pickings. He likes going for those just on the fringes of Christianity—just inside or just outside.

But if you've been a Christian for ages, you're really keen, you know all the answers (and are therefore unbearable), don't think you're immune. Proud people are the Devil's little delicacy.

What can the Devil do?

The Devil can tempt you but not force you

The Devil is a tempter. He can do no more. He can suggest that you do things, but he can't force you into doing them. His suggestions may be shouted at you. They may be terribly attractive, with all sorts of 'special offers', 'free gifts', and sales gimmicks like 'this month only' and 'while stocks last'.

But they're still only suggestions. If you do what he suggests, it's your decision. It's up to you.

When Paul writes to the Christians at Corinth, he tells them to get their act together:

> No temptation has seized you except what is common to man. And God is faithful; he will not let you be tempted beyond what you can bear. But when you are tempted, he will also provide a way out so that you can stand up under it (1 Corinthians 10:13).

So Paul is telling them not to be so wet and pathetic. 'You

don't *have* to cave in.' No one can use the excuse: 'The Devil made me do it.'

He is also saying that God lets us be tempted, so that we will grow as Christians. There's a reason behind it. It may not be very nice at the time, but it's good for you.

The Devil can blind people, but not permanently

> The God of this age [that's the Devil] has blinded the minds of unbelievers, so that they cannot see the light of the Gospel of the glory of Christ, who is the image of God (2 Corinthians 4:4).

This is Paul telling those Christians at Corinth what the Devil does to non-Christians. He blinds them. Well, he blinds their minds. So they can't understand the Gospel.

Quite often, I explain the Gospel to people and they haven't a clue what I'm on about. Sometimes that's because I explain it badly. Sometimes though, it's like talking to a brick wall. They *cannot* understand. No chance. They've got a mind malfunction. The Devil has turned off that bit of their mind which deals with spiritual things.

But God can throw the switch. That's why it's so important that we pray for our non-Christian friends. Ask God to flick the switch, to get their minds working to understand spiritual things. God's got to do that before you'll ever get them to understand what you're on about.

The Devil can possess people, but not Christians

There are some pretty ghoulish films around where people get possessed by demons. (It's probably best to think of demons as soldiers in the Devil's army.) Jesus came across lots of people who were possessed by demons, and he sorted them out.

Sometime, look at Mark 5:1–20 and see the amazing

authority Jesus had over demons. Demons? No problem for Jesus. He has total control over them. Demons do what Jesus tells them to (usually to clear off).

But note that 'possession' only takes place when the person wants that to happen or gets involved in occult-type things, like seances. Steer well clear of all occult practices. Don't touch them with a barge pole. You're dabbling with forces the power of which you wouldn't imagine.

And today, people can be possessed by demons. Some people go a bit overboard on all this. You know: every illness is caused by a demon; every setback in life is because Satan is after you; every sinful desire is because of an evil spirit in me. Some people see demons under every cup and saucer. We need to be realistic: the Bible shows us that demons do exist and they can possess people.

But not you—if you're a Christian. That's because a Christian is someone in whom Christ rules. And if your body is a 'Temple of the Holy Spirit' (1 Corinthians 6:19), there's no room for the Devil.

Don't be over-confident about it though. Take care, stay close to God, and don't play around with the Devil.

The Devil can confuse, but not destroy

> The Spirit clearly says that in later times some will abandon the faith and follow deceiving spirits and things taught by demons (1 Timothy 4:1).

Letters like 1 and 2 Timothy and Titus are full of warnings about those inside and outside the church, spurred on by the Devil, who teach wrong and confusing things. They cause confusion and division in the church. The early leaders Paul was writing to are given a very clear instruction on how to deal with them. There's no mucking around with these false teachers. Look for example at the following:

> But avoid foolish controversies and genealogies and
> arguments and quarrels about the law, because these are
> unprofitable and useless. Warn a divisive person once,
> and then warn him a second time. After that, have
> nothing to do with him. You may be sure that such a man
> is warped and sinful; he is self condemned (Titus 3:9–11).

But they won't destroy the church. God won't allow that.
They will muck up some people, and make them useless
for God. But the church will survive. More of all this in
Chapter 11.

The Devil can be ferocious, but he's also on a lead.
And the lead is held by God. And God has very strong
hands. Read Job, chapter 1. Here the Devil (or 'Satan' as
he's called here), asks for God's permission before he
ruins Job's life. He then makes Job's life fall apart. Nasty
stuff, but God is still in charge. And Job came to realise
that. The Devil can only go so far. God is in charge.

How to treat the Devil

In the Bible the Devil is portrayed as a snake. That's a
useful picture to have in mind.

How would you treat a snake? I've got a morbid fascination for the things. We were in Kenya once, and I just
had to go to the snake park in Nairobi. In this place
they've got all the most poisonous ones, in an open,
smooth-sided pit.

Riveting! And scary. I suppose I've got a healthy disrespect for snakes. I don't like them. I'm very cautious of
them.

Do the same with the Devil. Don't develop a liking for
him. Be very cautious. Exercise a healthy disrespect.

Put yourself in the Devil's shoes, just for a moment. He
doesn't like being looked at. But sometimes he can turn
that to his advantage. If a sensible study of the Devil turns
into fascination, you're in big trouble, and he's pulling
you in, like being pulled into a machine by your sleeve
caught in its gears. Don't get too close. Take care.

The future of the Devil

Looks bleak. But there's no need to feel sorry for him.

It all goes back to the Cross.

That central event of all human history was also the central event in the history of the Devil. It's all a bit complicated, and we'll have eternity to get to understand it. But one of the things that was happening was that Jesus and the Devil were having a battle.

The mother of all battles.

And thankfully for you and me, Jesus won. The Devil has been dealt a death blow. He's not dead yet. He's in his death throes. And as with any animal that's fatally wounded he can be particularly nasty as he thrashes around. But his end is sure and certain—final defeat and destruction, as all evil, and evil beings, are finally eradicated from the universe.

But remember: that is in the future. Right now, we have a dangerous opponent.

Digging in

I'm not suggesting any more things for you to do here. Don't study the Devil. Just move on to the next chapter.

11

The old master versus the cheap plastic imitation — spotting counterfeits, forgeries and other fakes

Don't try to understand it right now . . .

A few years ago I was walking down the High Street of the town I lived in, with a good friend of mine called Mark. We were stopped by a young man wanting to know if we'd like to give some money to missionary work.

We got talking and it transpired that this 'missionary' was a member of the Unification Church, i.e. he was a Moonie. As soon as the penny dropped I waded in with 'Well we're Christians and we think you're wrong in a number of ways...' Mark started fidgeting nervously as the Moonie (no relation!) aggressively brought the conversation to a halt.

'Next time,' Mark suggested, 'you ought to be a little more subtle.' Dead right!

You find these new religious movements, or 'cults', everywhere. Jehovah's Witnesses knock at your door, smart looking young men from the Church of Jesus Christ and Latter Day Saints (i.e. the Mormons) call around, and New Age thinking is spreading like gangrene wherever you look.

Some of them are very attractive, and seem to be saying the sorts of things that your minister in church would agree with.

But that's just it. They are made to look like the real thing. But they are counterfeits. They are fakes, forgeries.

This chapter is a crash course in how to spot the counterfeits. Just as an expert in £10 notes would look for certain things in a possibly counterfeit £10 note, so we can look for certain things which would help us to spot a counterfeit Christianity.

This doesn't just apply to the more obvious cults. If you look back at the history of present-day cults, many had close connections with mainline Christianity and were led away by charismatic personalities with increasingly weird and unreliable ideas.

So the check-points that follow give us a standard against which to measure what the cults are teaching, and to help us assess some to the new teachings we find in our own churches today. It's all going to get a little bit theological. So if you're getting bored or out of your depth, don't worry. Just skip on to Chapter 12 and come back to this some other time.

Spotting the Counterfeits—
Questions to Ask

Do they believe that Jesus was 100% God and 100% man?

Many counterfeits have funny ideas about Jesus. They may think he's not unique, or that he's not God or that he's not man. So if you come across a counterfeit, find out what they think about Jesus.

Christianity says that Jesus was 100 per cent God and 100 per cent man, all in one. Impressive, huh? Don't try to understand it right now. Just believe it, because it's important: a lot of other things hang on this statement about the nature of Jesus.

Do they believe in the Trinity?

I've already mentioned the Trinity in Chapter 6. That is: we believe there is one God, in three persons, each of whom is 100 per cent God: God the Father, God the Son, and God the Holy Spirit. So you've got a three in one God.

I don't know of a counterfeit Christianity which believes in the Trinity. And many distortions of Christianity emphasise one person of the Trinity and seem to exclude all the others. So you get versions of Christianity which ignore the Holy Spirit, or versions of Christianity which only ever mention the Holy Spirit.

So, check them out on the Trinity. Again, it's hard to understand (well, impossible, actually!), but that's how the Bible reveals God to us, so we therefore believe it.

Do they believe in the Bible?

Many counterfeits believe in the Bible and then add their own books to it. So, their holy books are the Bible and (for example), the Divine Light (for the Moonies), the Pearl of Great Price (for the Jehovah's Witnesses), the Book of Mormon (for the Mormons), etc. The Bible is not unique, they say. It's not the main way God speaks to us.

Counterfeits within the Church begin to say similar things about the Bible. They say it's not *sufficient*. In other words, they say the Bible is not sufficient to tell us all that we need to know about God and his demands on us. They say that we need some special extra revelation of God.

Chapter 5 makes it clear that the Bible is God speaking to us, and it's *all we need* to know about God and what he wants us to do with our lives.

Do they believe in sin?

Many counterfeits say that mankind is basically good with occasional bad bits. They don't believe that we were born with a natural inbuilt tendency to screw things up.

And if you were to ask them 'What's the problem with mankind?', they might talk about society, they might talk about the need to be put in touch with your real self, or the need to meet God, (sounds promising...), but they wouldn't talk about sin.

Sin has got a lot to answer for. Sin is the root cause of all the problems in the world.

Sin is the reason Jesus came, and died for you and for me.

The trouble is, counterfeits are very good at ignoring sin, or playing it down.

Christianity, however, takes sin very seriously indeed.

Do they believe in Jesus' death?

Jesus died for your sin and mine, so that we could be forgiven and be reunited with God. Jesus' death is the only way that we are going to get to Heaven.

The Cross is the central point of Christianity. It's in the gold medal position, but a counterfeit will remove it from the rostrum.

Now for a few things about the dangers of counterfeits.

Counterfeits are dangerous because truth is important

Does this all really matter? I mean, we don't want to get into a big witch hunt, do we? Surely we should all be entitled to our own opinions? And anyway, who's to say we're right and they're wrong?

I guess your friends at school may say that kind of thing. It's very popular today to say 'You believe what you believe, and I'll believe what I believe.' To say that truth doesn't matter is a very handy way of fobbing off Christians.

But we're not just chucking around ideas like you might juggling balls at a party. We're talking about God. If God exists, some statements about him are right and some are wrong. And if God is going to come and end the world, if he cares that much about us, then whether your ideas about God are right or wrong, is very important.

Counterfeits are dangerous, because the Gospel is important

The Gospel is the way that human beings get sorted out with God. It's the way we get saved and go to heaven. And counterfeits muck it up.

That can mean some people who ought to get saved, don't. This is getting heavy, because nothing is more important than that.

Counterfeits are dangerous because how we live is important

Counterfeits usually lead to bad behaviour. God says the way we live is very important. He gives us guidelines for living. And he expects us to keep to them.

Counterfeits twist and distort those guidelines, like an

old window which gives you an odd idea of what it is you are looking at through it. So counterfeits lead you to break God's laws, because they are not telling you what God's laws are. Bad news.

So what do I DO?

First, **get back to basics**. Counterfeits go on from the basics. The Bible is always telling us to go back to basics. Go back to the Gospel time and time again. It won't be boring. It can't be. The Gospel is at the heart of everything you are and do for God. So don't forget it, and always go back there, especially if you think you may have a counterfeit on your hands.

Forgers copy the real thing. Counterfeit specialists know the real thing brilliantly well so that they can spot the fake. So should we.

Second, **help each other**. Get your friends to help you. Help them. Help each other to be sound in what you believe and good in how you behave. That's what Christian friends are for.

Third, **crave good teaching**. Paul is always telling Timothy, when confronted by counterfeits, to carry on his good teaching. For example:

> Do your best to present yourself to God as one approved, a workman who does not need to be ashamed and who correctly handles the Word of truth (2 Timothy 2:15).

In other words good teaching is Bible teaching. Teaching where the Bible is handled properly and understood rightly. Crave it. Go to a church where you get it. Go to a youth group and the school Christian Union where you get it. Read books where you get it. Even listen to sermons on tapes where you get it. There's no substitute for good Bible teaching.

Finally, **don't mix it**. Don't think that you can persuade them single-handed. They are both deceivers and deceived—and they could make mincemeat out of you. The wise course is to steer clear. Your faith is at stake. You wouldn't try sorting out a minefield on your own would you? You'd leave it to the experts. This is a minefield. So stay out, and leave it to the experts.

I hope that wasn't all too heavy. Congratulations on getting through it. The important thing is to know your own faith well, so you know what you believe, and therefore recognise when others believe something different.

DIGGING IN

1. Read 1 Timothy, 2 Timothy and Titus. They aren't very long, so it won't take you ages. As you read these, look out for the counterfeits that Paul is worried about. Note down what they believed or did that was wrong, and also what Paul tells Timothy and Titus to do about them.

2. Get a bit of paper and write down what you believe about the following. It will help you to be clear in your own mind.

    a. What is the Bible?
    b. What happened at the Cross?
    c. What is sin, and how does it affect me?
    d. Was Jesus just a man?
    e. How do you get to Heaven?

3. Ask your youth leader to do some sessions on what Christians believe and one or two on the cults.

4. Read one of the many books on the cults, to find out a little bit more about them. Ask your minister or youth leader what they recommend.

Sex — just one of God's great ideas (but handle with care)

To be really safe you need to wear a wet suit

You can't avoid it. Wherever you go: adverts, TV, films, fashion. They're all shouting at you 'Sex is good for you'. We live in a world where sex is talked about, practised, paraded, flaunted. Sex is the answer (so we're told). It solves all your problems. It sells things. It satisfies. It fulfils. Some thing, sex. Or is it all a big con? Has our sex-mad society just gone too far? Is sex really the be-all and end-all? Is sex all that it's made out to be?

I used to live with a couple of friends, one of whom, Colin, slept with his girlfriend, Jenny. One morning at breakfast, Colin said to me 'You know Phil, sex isn't all it's cracked up to be. Jenny tries her best, but I'm bored with it.'

Pity. Because God is very keen on sex. He wants us to enjoy it. Sex is very important to God. Let's find out more.

Nice one, God

Yes that's right. Sex is God's idea. He thought of it. I'm always amused to read the first commandment God gave to Adam and Eve:

> So God created man in his own image, in the image of God he created him; male and female he created them. God blessed them and said to them, 'Be fruitful and increase in number; fill the earth and subdue it' (Genesis 1:27–28).

The first thing God tells Adam and Eve to do is to go and have sex. Don't let anyone fool you into thinking that God is anti-sex. No. He's all for it.

But some people say 'You're kidding! God hates sex. What about all those commands "Thou shalt not commit adultery". "Do not fornicate". "God will judge the homosexual"? God hates sex.'

No. These commands in the Bible are there to stop us *mis*using sex. Do adultery (i.e. sex when somebody's married but they aren't your husband or wife), fornication (or sexual immorality—i.e. sex outside marriage) and homosexuality sound like the use of sex or the misuse of sex? God is all for sex. In fact it's so important to him that he gives us guidelines to make sure that we use it properly. He doesn't want it mucked up.

Not so long ago, a number of friends borrowed our car and crashed it for us. I do quite like cars, but I'm afraid I can't get worked up about them. Our car is always dirty, and it doesn't really bother me when people crash it for us. It's a bit of a nuisance, but not something to get heartbroken about. They're only things, and not that important.

But if someone was to do something to Anna, Katherine or Christopher (my family), then I would get very worked up. They are incredibly important to me. I guess that's because they are people and not things. And they are very close to my heart.

Sex isn't just a thing either. It's not in the 'car' category. It's not just a physical act, like press-ups or eating. It's something that happens between and involves, intimately, two people. And because people are important to God, sex, as far as God is concerned, is very precious, and worth looking after.

Where sex lives

If you have a hamster, you really ought to look after it. It needs food and water, some newspaper, woodshavings or whatever to make a nest, and something to gnaw on. And it needs a cage, to protect it from your cat, and to protect your parents' furniture from its teeth. Hamsters need homes.

God wants to protect you, and to protect his brilliant gift of sex, so he has made a home for it, where it can be used and enjoyed to its full. The home for sex is marriage. If sex wasn't so important, it wouldn't matter quite so much if we abused it. If sex wasn't such good fun, God wouldn't bother with providing a good home for it. But sex is brilliant. It's a good thing. It's worth protecting. It's worth keeping in its natural environment—the marriage of a man to a woman.

So that's why God sets guidelines for our use of sex. He wants us to enjoy it so he gives rules for our enjoyment. God wants to protect us from the consequences of the misuse of sex (e.g. AIDS, lack of stability in relationships, misunderstanding of what sex is for, and things like that), so he gives us the best possible home for sex so that we can enjoy it to its full.

God is not a cosmic killjoy. He's not a wrinkly old man perching on a cloud, shouting 'Stop it' as soon as he sees us beginning to enjoy ourselves. Sex is his idea, and he wants us to enjoy it. So he gives us instructions on how to use this brilliant present.

Why wait?

There are loads of reasons to wait until you're married. Here are a few of them:

1. Spiritual reasons

If you're a Christian, the main reason to wait is because God tells you to. And God knows best, doesn't he? After all, since he invented it, he ought to have the best idea of how it should be used.

Sex outside marriage is disobedient to God. You can try and argue your way out of it. You can try and convince yourself that it's OK. But the bottom line is that sex outside marriage is being disobedient to God. So it will damage your walk with God.

That's not irreversible. You can stop, change your direction, ask God to forgive you, and he will. But let's not hide the fact that sex outside marriage is being disobedient to God.

2. Physical reasons

What if you get pregnant? I know a number of teenage girls who've got pregnant. In every case it's changed their lives. One had an abortion, and found it quite an appalling experience. Incredibly, she got pregnant again a few weeks later, only this time she kept the baby. And it's changed her life.

What if you catch an STD (i.e. a sexually transmitted disease)? That can change your life too. Unlikely? Who are you kidding? No contraceptive is 100 per cent successful, and condoms certainly aren't a sure fire safeguard against AIDS. You need to wear a wet suit to be safe. They're no longer calling it safe sex, are they? It's saf*er* sex.

How many STDs do you think there are? 5? 10? 20? At the last count, over 50, and rising. And people who know about these things say that if you've slept with someone before your wedding night, on that night you're exposing your wife/husband not only to any STDs that you have, but also to those that your previous partners had, and their previous partners, and so on. So as far as STDs are concerned, you could be sleeping with thousands of people, and in one sexual act could be passing on several different STDs to your husband or wife.

That's not fantasy. It's fact. Do you want to be the bearer of disease on your wedding night?

3. Emotional reasons

Losing your virginity is still a very significant event for most people. You do it only once. Many people regret losing it in the back of a car, on the sofa, or in the sand dunes, to someone they hardly knew and now don't even send a Christmas card to.

Anna and I waited. It was very tough going, waiting until our wedding night. A real struggle. We almost blew it a number of times, but we hung in there and waited. We wanted God's best for us—and it was worth it.

Sex also sets going all sorts of emotions. That's why God wants it to live in the home of a permanent, stable, marriage, where those emotional needs can hopefully be met. If you see sex just as a physical act, you're ignoring a huge area of the significance of sex for human beings. This isn't easy. I'm as aware as you are that there are enormous pressures on you to give it a go. I just want to point out that there are actually very good reasons for waiting. And they are far better reasons than those given for saying 'yes'.

What about NOW?

'It's all very well for you. You're married.' Yes, I am, but Anna and I were going out for six years before we got married. You *can* wait. It *is* possible.

And during that time, I would go along to the 'Relationships' talk at our youth group, ignore all the 'marriage' stuff and long to see their answer to the only really important question for a teenage bloke—'How far can I go?'

Wrong question. I wanted someone to say 'Go this far and no further'. Dummy. If they had said that, I would have gone right up to the line, and then failed to stop. No, I thank God for the wise old birds who gave us good principles to go on. Principles like these:

1. Go slow

Most young people think it's OK, even wise, to hold hands, kiss, and hug on your first night out. Well, if you do that, unless you're very self-controlled, you're heading for the scrap heap. What's the hurry? Why are you kissing her/him anyway?

Slow down! I know I'm very backwards in coming forwards, but it took us ages before we even held hands. And we remember the occasion. How cute! But given the difficulty we had in holding ourselves back later on, I'm very glad to be backward.

2. Giving or getting?

What is sex anyway? Do you want sex for what you give or for what you can get from it?

It's a bit of both, but the emphasis must be on the

90

giving. It's a physical expression of the total self-giving of one person to another that's called marriage. In sex therefore, we aim to please our partner.

A lot of sex these days is about getting. 'I want' is the main reason for sleeping together or the quick encounter in the corner of the rec (leaving the used condom on the grass for others to clear up). That wrecks what sex should really be. God intended that we should give, not just get. Bear that in mind and it should help you take sex more seriously.

3. Arousal or affection?

There's a thin dividing line here. We naturally want to express our affection physically, and so we might hold hands, kiss, etc. Ultimately, sex is a wonderful expression of affection. The problem comes when this turns to arousal, and when you just do things to arouse yourself or your partner. When you start playing with something your partner has and you don't, then it's past the time to stop, but you probably won't be able to.

But thankfully God has arranged things so that girls *tend* to get worked up less easily than blokes. Well anyway, whoever is less worked up is in the best position to be firm and strong and to stop things progressing when they're getting out of control. When the talking stops and the breathing starts, try starting to talk to each other, perhaps about the sermon on Sunday...That should do the trick! But if not, try the Common Agricultural Policy. And if that doesn't work, then simply get up, sit up, stand up or do *something* to get yourselves out of the situation.

4. Flee the temptation

The best way to deal with temptation is to run away from it: 'Flee the evil desires of youth, and pursue righteousness, faith, love and peace, along with those who call on the Lord out of a pure heart' (2 Timothy 2:22).

So many young people do the opposite with sex. After your parents have gone to bed you lie down on the sofa together, watching the late night movie. That's really stupid. You sit on the bed together, listening to records. Who are you kidding? You go on holiday together, just the two of you, and share an apartment with one bedroom. Sheer stupidity.

And disobedient—we're supposed to run away from temptation, not to walk into it with open arms thinking we are going to beat it.

Let's be positive about it. When you see a problem coming, tell your boyfriend/girlfriend, and then walk away from it.

5. It's a relationship
And all relationships can't just be built on physical arousal and sex. You're more than just a body. Relationships are based on getting to know the person concerned.

So work on doing things together, on talking to each other about all sorts of subjects. Humans are complex beings, not just sexual objects, and they take a lot of getting to know. A marriage based on sexual attraction and sexual activity alone is on shaky foundations.

The big picture
Sex is part of a much bigger picture. If you were to examine the eyes of Tom Cruise, Michelle Pfeiffer, or whoever it is that you have on your bedroom wall, at close range, you may find them intriguing, even fascinating. You may want eyes like those. But you can only really appreciate them, when you look at the whole picture.

It's the same with sex. Sex can't be seen just on its own, in isolation. Look at the whole picture. That might help you to appreciate it, and therefore to treat it with the respect it deserves.

DIGGING IN

1. If you have a boy or girlfriend, ask them to read this chapter, and then talk about it with them.

2. Check out:

> Romans 1:18–27;
> 1 Corinthians 6:18–20;
> Colossians 3:5–6;
> 1 Thessalonians 4:3–8;
> 1 John 1:8–10.

   Write down in your notebook what these verses tell you about how God views sex. Compare what he thinks with what you think. Then talk to him about it, and ask him to help you to see it his way.

3. Ask your youth leaders to help you conduct a confidential survey of your group's sexual attitudes.

13

Going, going, gone
— out with a non-Christian

You may be able to cope with a train spotter...

Dear Phil and Anna,

Sorry I haven't been down to the youth group the last few weeks, but I've just got to tell you about this fantastic boy I met at a party last month.

His name is Dave and he's in the 6th form at The Oaks. He's got such a lovely voice and he's really tall and good looking. And he's got a car, this really cute Mini which he's got resprayed. I'm hoping I'll get him along to church soon. I'm working on him. He says he's interested in Christianity, so I'm really praying God will work in his life.

See you soon,
Loads of luv,
Juli

Sounds familiar? All over the country, thousands of Christian teenagers are going out with boy or girlfriends who aren't Christians.

Is that a good idea? Does it matter if you, a Christian, go out with someone who isn't a Christian? Right now, you may be going out with someone who isn't a Christian. Or you may wish you were. Wouldn't it be nice if this book could say 'That's great! That's fine. Pairing up with a non-Christian—no problem!' But I'm afraid I have to say the exact opposite.

First, what does the Bible say about going out with a non-Christian? Is it OK? Is it OK sometimes? Is it sometimes wrong? Is it always wrong? What does the Bible say?

The short answer is, 'nothing'. At least, nothing directly. That's mainly because people didn't 'go out' in those days, so if Paul had written a letter about 'going out with non-Christians', they wouldn't have had a clue what he was on about.

Sometimes people say you shouldn't go out with a non-Christian, and they quote 2 Corinthians 6:14 at you: 'Do not be yoked together with unbelievers'. Unfortunately, that's all about mixing worship of God with worship of idols. I guess you could apply the principle to going out with a non-Christian, but there's no specific command here. God isn't saying 'Don't go out with a non-Christian'. At least not here, in so many words.

But I want to suggest that if you look at what the Bible says about being a Christian, and if you're wise about how you live your life, you won't even consider going out with someone who isn't a Christian.

It's not train-spotting

If you think you can go out with a non-Christian and survive as a Christian, I'm afraid you've got a completely wrong idea of what Christianity is.

If you're going out with someone and they like train-spotting (would you go out with *anyone* who liked train-spotting?), and you didn't, that may just enrich your relationship as you learn about British Rail locomotives. But the thing about train-spotting is that it's just a hobby. It's a spare-time activity. I don't want to be harsh on people who wear anoraks, but there's more to life than train-spotting.

But there isn't any more to life than Christianity. Christianity *is* life. It's everything. It's no hobby or spare-time interest. Christianity takes you over—or at least it *should* do. It affects everything. The lot. You may be able to cope with an average train-spotter. But how about someone whose ideas, language, thinking, attitudes and concerns are all focused on trains? How about someone whose whole life revolves around train-spotting?

Christians, too, are people who have been taken over, not by trains, but by God. As a Christian you are a different being, a different creature from a non-Christian. So you'd be really unwise to think you could go out with a non-Christian, and have any real depth to your relationship.

Mix and match

There aren't any specific Bible verses saying 'Don't go out with a non-Christian', but there are plenty suggesting that it pollutes you. God wants to create a people who are set aside for him—his special people. In the Old Testament these people were the people of Israel. In the New Testament it's the Church—i.e. Christians.

In the Old Testament God is always going on at them not to marry people outside the people of Israel, because that would pollute the people of God. It would water down their commitment and ruin their faith:

> Then Ezra the priest stood up and said to them, 'You have been unfaithful; you have married foreign women, adding to Israel's guilt' (Ezra 10:10).

It's a similar idea today with the Church. Marrying people outside the Church introduces stresses and strains which pull people away from God. And it's just the same if you're going out with someone who's not a Christian.

Marriage on the horizon

I started going out with Anna when she was 15 and I was 18. We had no thought of getting married when we started going out, but just look at us now! So you could start going out with someone who isn't a Christian, just for a bit of light-hearted fun, but then fall hopelessly in love with them and end up marrying them.

I don't think you can be too careful with this kind of thing, because your faith, your eternal life, and your usefulness to God are at stake.

Second best?

Going out with a non-Christian is second best. That's not to say that they're second-best people of course. Rather, that a relationship between two Christians will be a better, deeper one, because you'll have in common the most important thing in life: your relationship with God.

You'll have in common the fact that you are new beings, that you've had your sin forgiven, and that you are heading for Heaven. You can go to church and other Christian meetings together. You can talk about these things together, and understand each other. You can pray together, and read the Bible together.

A relationship with a non-Christian would be missing all that. That's second best. But it's worse than that. Because going out with a non-Christian is putting that person before God. So you're not just settling for second best. You're making God second best.

Be honest with yourself

You're going out with someone who isn't a Christian. You may (like Juli at the beginning), see it as a great evangelistic opportunity, but usually, in fact almost always, the Christian gets clobbered.

If I look back at all the Christian teenagers I know who have fallen away, the biggest single reason is that they started going out with a non-Christian. In fact, in my experience going out with a non-Christian accounts for more casualties than all the other reasons put together. It's all a bit like water and fire: either the water will put out the fire, or the fire will dry up the water. You can't have the two together. If you're a Christian, your faith is the fire, and very often it's a young fire, just getting going, and easily put out by a bucketful of non-Christian water.

This is a dangerous business. Your love for each other, or your love for God. Either your love for God will fizzle to make room for your love for each other, or your love for each other will dry up to make room for your love for God.

Are you going out with anyone? And if not, why not?

'It's OK for you Phil. You're married, to a Christian. But where I live, all the Christian blokes are two years younger than me, wet and spotty. Who'd want to go out with any of them?'

Well, quite. But I do know something of the pressures to have a boy/girlfriend. Before I started going out with Anna, all my friends at school claimed to have girlfriends. Looking back on it, I'm sure they didn't, but I believed them at the time. So once, just once, I told them I had a girlfriend called Carol. That made me feel accepted by them, normal. Carol never existed, but when you're under pressure, an imaginary girlfriend can be almost as useful as the real thing.

It's all a lie though, isn't it? There are loads and loads of people who aren't going out with anyone. In many youth groups, couples are in the minority. You don't *have* to go out with anyone. And if you don't have a boy/girlfriend, that doesn't make you into some sort of mutant. Nor does it mean that you're ugly, with bad breath, BO and greasy hair.

Most people end up getting married (even the most unlikely candidates!). But that doesn't mean you have to have a perpetual boy/girlfriend on the go until you do. Youth groups, of all places, ought to be the kind of places where it's OK *not* to have a boy/girlfriend. (And also the kind of place where you're accepted even if you are ugly, with bad breath, BO and greasy hair!).

Some of the Christians I most admire are those who have put God first, even above getting a boy/girlfriend, even above getting married to someone. And for many of those people, they've ended up getting married in the end, to someone quite brilliant.

But it is possible that you will end up 'on the shelf'. That's tough. Really tough. If you think that you may be heading that way, remember that God loves you more than you can ever imagine. He knows what you think and feel. He knows what you want. He knows about boy and girlfriends. But what he wants is for you to put him first. Leave the boy/girlfriend and getting married bit up to God. He's well capable of looking after all that. And put

God first. That is sure-fire, guaranteed, the best way of being given the best boy/girlfriend you could possibly imagine.

Put God first. Trust him that he knows best about boy and girlfriends, husbands and wives. Trust him that he loves you, and that he will give you the very best, and that he knows exactly what that is.

DIGGING IN

1. Think: what can you do to make your youth group the sort of place where it's OK *not* to have a boy/girlfriend? Talk to your friends about it, and talk to your youth leaders about it.

2. Go for a walk on your own, and have a think about why you want to have a boy or girlfriend. Talk this over with God. Be honest with him about how you feel and what you really want. Ask God to help you to put him first in this area of your life now and in the future.

3. Check out:

    Matthew 6:33–34;
    Hebrews 12:1–3;
    1 Peter 1:13–16.

    How does what God says in these verses relate to going out with people? Write down what you think in your note-book.

Grab, grab, grab
— living in the material world

...spending more and more money to look acceptable

What kind of world is it where you judge someone by the car they drive, the trainers they wear, the size of their CD collection and where they went on holiday last year? A pretty sick one.

Those things though, are important to us, aren't they? If you're a normal teenager, the name on your trainers is very important, as are the number of eyelets on your DMs, the label on the outside of your jacket, and the pose-factor of your hi-fi.

We've all been conned

It's got to be Nike or Reebok, Naf-Naf or Next. And who'd be seen dead in a pair of Woolies own-brand jeans or with a Dixons own-brand walkman? At least, that's what we think our friends think. And they think that's what we think. But do they? And do you? We may just have conned each other into spending more and more money to look acceptable, when actually, if we're honest with each other, we've been conned.

Advertisers have made a very good job of making their product indispensable. And the teenage market is a huge one. The advertisers have made you a target. They recognised a long time ago that teenagers are pretty rich (yes you are—honest!). And they are now particularly good at getting you to buy their products—clothes, music, drinks, and more.

Money talks

You may have a bank account. You probably notice the cars that people drive and the houses they live in. You take note of the expensive hi-fi, the Nicam TV and the hi-band camcorder. You probably know how much they cost. We therefore pigeon-hole people into 'rich', 'not quite so rich', 'stinking rich', 'not as rich as me', etc. Money has become the language that we all speak.

Sad, isn't it? Because God doesn't speak that language at all.

More, more, more

Money, and the things it buys, never satisfies.

You say to yourself, 'If only I get that new CD' or 'When I have that motorbike', or 'As soon as I have that jacket, life will be complete and I'll be satisfied'. You've got to be joking! I'll give you a week before you're wanting more albums, a bigger bike, and other clothes. The simple fact is that no matter how many things we have, they won't satisfy. We'll always want more.

That's good news for the advertisers, and bad news for us.

Rich, but foolish?

Jesus told a story about a rich man who died suddenly, and God said to him:

> 'You fool! This very night your life will be demanded from you. Then who will get what you have prepared for yourself?' This is how it will be with anyone who stores up things for himself but is not rich towards God (Luke 12:20–21).

Here Jesus is telling us that a life based on the material world is pretty short-sighted. You may do very well here on Earth. You may be 'successful' and rich. People here may think you're a bit of a hero. You could even drive a Rolls. And Jesus says, you can be a hero to today's world, but if you leave God out of it, you're a fool.

This world is not all that there is. When you die, that's *not* the end. You (your soul) go on to eternity, and you meet God face to face. Then what's he going to say to you? He could say, if you've been taking him seriously during your life 'Hello my good friend, well done'. Or, if you've ignored him, he could say 'You fool'.

Don't be a fool. There is more to life than this material world.

Money, money, money

Do you want to get rich? Do you love money? It's attractive isn't it? But dangerous for the Christian, and dangerous for the Church too.

The Devil would love us to fall in love with money. That way, he could divert us from the Gospel, and make us spend our time trying to get rich. Getting rich? Sounds nice. It's not necessarily bad, but it can be addictive, and there are more important things in life.

That's some of what the Bible tells us about the dangers of materialism. But more positively, what should be our attitude to possessions and money?

Thinking positively

First, get it straight that none of it's yours. It's all God's. You have use of it for the time being, but it's on loan from God. So don't get too attached to it.

Be prepared to lend things to people, and don't worry if they come back damaged or if they don't come back at all. Don't worry about getting your old records scratched or your leather jacket stained. They're not really yours anyway.

Serving God and money?

If you've got a Bible could you look up Luke 16:1–15? This is about how we use our money for God.

Jesus is saying that 'You cannot serve God and money'. You'll either serve one or the other. Which are you serving?

If you're serving God, what should your attitude to money be? Basically this: 'Use all your money to serve God.' And in particular, use all your money to serve the Gospel and to help other people to become Christians. That's not saying 'Give it all away'. And this isn't saying it's wrong to own things. But we've got to be careful what we spend our money on, and ask questions like, 'Is this extravagant?' and, 'If I buy this, will it help others to become Christians?'

There's nothing wrong with spending money on pleasure and enjoyment either, but spend it carefully. Do stop before you buy your 101st CD and ask yourself 'Do I really *need* this?' Ask the same question before you upgrade your bike to a Harley Davidson, and before you buy your fourth pair of jeans. The answer may be, 'Yes, I do need it'. But it's probably more likely to be, 'No'.

Do ask how you can best use your money to serve God on Earth. It may best be used by giving it to some organisation, to help them spread the Gospel, or you may want to give it to relieve suffering. Or you may want to keep it, because it will help you spread the Gospel among your friends. All this involves beginning to think about giving, so let's do more of that now.

Giving it all away?

If there's one thing that amazes non-Christians, it's why Christians should give money away. Non-Christians may give away their loose change, but they fail to see why Christians should give away significant amounts of their own money. In the material world, people don't do that.

And right now you are in a brilliant position. You don't have many responsibilities and not very many commitments. So now is the very best time to sort out your giving and to lay down principles which you'll try to keep to in later life. Check out 'Digging in' at the end of this chapter for doing something practical about this.

> Each man should give what he has decided in his heart to give, not reluctantly or under compulsion, for God loves a cheerful giver (2 Corinthians 9:7).

The Corinthian Christians were good at giving. Their attitude to their money was something like, 'Well it's not really mine anyway—it's on loan from God—so I'm only giving back to him what was his in the first place.'

God loves people who give. He loves people who give

themselves, their time and effort. He loves people who give their money.

It's a good principle always to give away at least one-tenth of what you get. The Old Testament people of God did it. But there's no rule. You don't have to. And you don't have to be bound by it—you could give a lot more!

Giving—once you get used to it, it's a great privilege, and God always, somehow, makes sure that you get back more than you give.

Who to?

Anna and I always give to Christian people or organisations. There are plenty of non-Christians to give to the non-Christian organisations. And we always give to our local church to support the work there. We like to give to organisations which are helping to spread the Gospel. And we like to limit the number of people and organisations we give to.

Give and pray

Giving to a few people and organisations also helps you to pray for them. If you give to, say, Tear Fund, make sure you get their 'Tear Times' and the prayer diary. Keep in touch and pray. You could ask for the prayer letter from a specific mission partner in a Third World country, so you could pray specifically for them. And why not save up and go and see them? We did, a few years ago. Our church was supporting a family who were missionaries in Uganda so we saved up and went to see them one summer holiday.

I can recommend it. And I think, so can they!

DIGGING IN

1. Why not sit down, write down your weekly income (pocket money, Saturday job, etc), and then decide how much you're going to give away? See what 10 per cent looks like. Can you give more? What can you give up so that you can give away more? Decide where it's going and in what proportions.

2. Make a list of the last five or ten significant things you bought for yourself. Against each one, note down why you bought it, and answer the question 'Would I buy it again?'

3. What is the *one* thing you would really love to have, right now? If it's the sort of thing which is a luxury rather than a necessity, seriously consider doing without it. Give the money you would have spent on it, to a worthwhile cause. And don't tell anyone what you've done. We don't give our money away in order to boast about our generosity.

Pressure points — living as a Christian in an anti-Christian world

Your mind gets used to it

Back in Chapter 1 I mentioned a friend of mine who invited me to his church youth group. That was a very important first step in me becoming a Christian. Iain also invited me to that first ever prayer meeting (the one I mentioned in Chapter 7). We did a lot together inside and outside the youth group. Our Christian faith grew together. We were committed and enthusiastic Christians. Yet over the last few years, Iain's faith seems to have dwindled and dried up. He'd still call himself a Christian, but it's all a bit of a struggle at the moment.

The sad thing is that a lot of Christians give up. They start off well, but find it tough going and in the end cave in. They either give up altogether, or they turn into a cross between a slug and a jelly: lethargic, hiding away when the heat's on, and no backbone at all.

One reason for this is that they haven't worked out ahead of time what being a Christian involves. Or maybe no one told them. So they hadn't twigged that being a Christian can be tough going. It's not a thing for wimps or cowards. And if you don't work out ahead of time how much something is going to cost, it may be that when you get down to paying for it, you can't afford it.

Being a Christian can be costly. But the rewards are out of this world. This chapter is an honest look at what being a Christian actually involves. If you're not a Christian, I hope it will help you to make a sensible decision. I don't want to put you off, but it's always wise to know what you are letting yourself in for.

Leaders of the opposition

The Bible talks about three things that try to drag us back from following Jesus. As we saw in Chapter 10, the Devil is one. The other two are what the Bible calls 'The world' and 'The flesh'. Together they conspire to prevent us from becoming Christians, and then if you do, they'll try to trip you up and make you useless as a Christian.

> As for you, you were dead in your transgressions and
> sins, in which you used to live when you followed the
> ways of this world and the ruler of the kingdom of the
> air, the spirit who is now at work in those who are
> disobedient. All of us also used to live among them at
> one time, gratifying the cravings of our sinful nature and
> following its desires and thoughts (Ephesians 2:1–3).

'The world' is not some classroom-illuminated globe,
but the Bible uses it to talk about humanity organised in
rebellion against God. So we can talk about 'The world's
attitude to this', or 'The world's way of thinking'—those
are thoughts and attitudes which human beings have
because we live in a world which leaves God out of it.

The 'Flesh', sometimes called our 'Sinful nature', is our
old, sinful self. When you became or become a Christian,
you are born again, but there's still the old you knocking
around, wanting you to do things you shouldn't.

Together, then, the world, the flesh and the Devil are
working against you, trying to get you to jack in your
relationship with God. That's the fight that's going on
under the surface. But how is it all seen?

Suicide time

Christians *are* different. We can't get away from the fact.
And that should mean that we act differently to our non-
Christian friends. If you are taking your Christian life
seriously, non-Christians will notice. You will stick out,
perhaps even like a sore thumb.

There's loads and loads that I could say here about the
difference that being a Christian should make to your
lifestyle. Try looking at the second half of any of the
letters in the New Testament if you want more details. For
example:

> Put to death, therefore, whatever belongs to your earthly
> nature: sexual immorality, impurity, lust, evil desires,
> and greed, which is idolatry. Because of these, the wrath
> of God is coming. You used to walk in these ways, in the

life you once lived. But now you must rid yourselves of all such things as these: anger, rage, malice, slander and filthy language from your lips. Do not lie to each other, since you have taken off your old self with its practices and have put on the new self, which is being renewed in knowledge in the image of its Creator (Colossians 3:5–10).

Strong stuff! Paul is telling us that to grow as a Christian, we've got to put a gun to our old selves and pull the trigger! We've got to kill off the habits which belong to our old, pre-Christian way of life, and grow the kind of deeds that belong to the new life.

That means, for example, that our sexual behaviour changes. All sex outside marriage stops; all thoughts of such stuff are cut out. Foul language, lies, and anger are out. In their place we have a really positive view of sex. We think sex is so brilliant that it's worth waiting for. We have new language. We speak well of others. We build them up. We tell the truth.

We may still slip back into old ways, but now they no longer rule our lives. They are the exception rather than the rule. And even if you only make a small attempt to do this you will be different, because most people don't even bother to try. Why should they? They've got no reason to.

Christians are different. And if that makes us stick out (like a healthy thumb!), so be it. It may make us unpopular with our non-Christian friends. They may wonder 'Are you real?', and choose to ignore us. Or they may well be attracted by a changed and changing Christian life, and be led to think and perhaps ask, 'Why?'

But if you're anything like me, then the last thing you want to do is to stick out as being different or peculiar. So the constant temptation is to conform and be just the same as everyone else. How can we keep going?

Here are some very brief outlines for how a Christian could handle some of the more difficult areas of living in our anti-Christian world.

Drinking

The Bible sees nothing wrong with drinking a little. But it sees a lot wrong with drinking a lot, and a lot wrong with under-age drinking. Buying drink when you're under 18 is breaking the law—even if everyone else is doing it, that doesn't make it all OK.

A lot of Christians drink too much. And there's a lot to be said for refusing to drink, to show others simply that you don't have to. And you could, also, not go to the pub for the same reason.

But if you are going to drink, make up your mind what your limit is, and stick to it. If it affects you, you've had too much, so stop. And don't have so much next time. Tell your friends at the start of the evening what your limit is. Thankfully, these days, people who think they are hard because of the amount they can hold down, are increasingly thought to be the numbskulls that they are.

Remember too, that drinking is not the only way that it's possible to enjoy yourself. With your group of Christian friends, work on ways of enjoying each others' company that don't depend on alcohol for the enjoyment factor.

Smoking

When you've been there at the bedside of your father-in-law as he dies of lung cancer caused at least in part by smoking, you tend to feel strongly about these things. It's a medically proven fact that smoking can kill you. Add to that the cost involved and you'll have to work hard to convince me that smoking is OK. And for the Christian, who should have a great respect for their body, because of who created it, there's no way you should kill it off by smoking. Don't do it.

Parties

Parties can be great fun. After all, what's Heaven going to be like? But you might just be invited to the sort of party that it would be unwise to go to. I'm not suggesting that all

Christians should automatically turn into couch potatoes. But I am suggesting that if you know that a party is likely to turn into a sordid, drunken orgy (or if one starts heading that way), why do you still want to go? Run away from temptation, not into it.

Films, TV, magazines and the like

Many films and TV programmes are really good, and worth watching for the sheer enjoyment of what has been produced.

But not all films are helpful for Christians. Again, the TV programmes you watch and the magazines you browse are important. The Biblical principle is that what goes into your brain determines what comes out. If you are filling your brain with lust, violence, greed, adultery, and the like, your brain gets used to it, develops a taste for it, and starts spewing it out on other people. It's far better to think about good things:

> Finally, brothers, whatever is true, whatever is noble, whatever is right, whatever is pure, whatever is lovely, whatever is admirable—if anything is excellent or praiseworthy—think about such things (Philippians 4:8).

How does the last TV programme you watched match up to that? Maybe you hit the bullseye. Or maybe you should alter your viewing and reading to fill your mind with good things.

Help!

Being a Christian can be great fun, and it's an incredible thrill to think that we are building up a relationship with the God of the Universe, and that he wants us to be involved in what he is doing. That's mind-blowing. But best of all is the fact that we are on our way to Heaven.

At the same time, being a Christian can be a big, long, grinding battle. There are great joys, yes, but it's tough too. A lot of it is 'Head down, go for the line' stuff, as we work away at being the best that we can be.

But don't get depressed. We're not supposed to be perfect straightaway. This is a marathon, not a sprint. And as in any race, it's the runner, i.e. you, who does the running. We don't just sit back and expect to be changed to be more like Jesus. We still have to do the work, but God helps us in it. He gives us the power to change, but it's us who do the changing.

So hang on in there. The rewards are terrific, both here, and in the world to come.

DIGGING   IN

1. Write down the three areas of your life where you are most under pressure from the non-Christian world. What can you do to stand up for Jesus more effectively?

2. Look up Galatians 5:1. What does that mean for you, today?

3. Team up with a Christian friend, and talk about how you can help each other to live Christian lives in today's non-Christian world.

16

Living with your parents

*...the only proof your mum needs that
something significant has happened!*

Most of us have got parents. And most teenagers still live with them. A proportion of those wish they didn't, and a much larger proportion have hassles with those older, unreasonable, misunderstanding and interfering people they have to share a house with.

This is an important area, especially if your parents aren't Christians. For many of us who become Christians as teenagers, our parents never quite get into the idea of their children being Christians. Still less do they get into the idea of their children staying Christians.

Many parents have a real fear that their kid will get involved in some weird cult, and they'll never see them again. So do assure them if you have just become a Christian, that it's all OK. You haven't just got involved in some cult, and you're still perfectly normal.

Get them to meet your youth leader or minister. Invite them around for a meal or whatever is appropriate where you live. At any rate, get your parents to see that you are with an ordinary bunch of Christians who can only do you good.

Getting on with Mum and Dad

It's a sobering fact that for almost all of us, our parents love us. I didn't quite twig just how much until we had children of our own. I know it all sounds really wet, but I love them incredibly. Vastly more than I thought I would. Vastly more than I thought I would be capable of. And I guess it could be the same with your parents and you.

God says children are to honour and obey their parents:

> Honour your father and your mother, so that you may live long in the land the Lord your God is giving you (Exodus 20:12).

> Children, obey your parents in the Lord, for this is right (Ephesians 6:1).

The general idea is that when in dependence on our parents, we are to obey them, and at all times we are to honour them. While you are still living at home, and your parents are providing for you, you are depending on them, and so you should be obedient, and honour them.

'What, even when they tell me that I have to be in at 10.00pm?' Yes.

'And even when they tell me what clothes I can and can't wear?' Yes.

But getting beyond those rules and regulations which annoy us so much, honouring our parents means, for example, talking to them. Tell them what you've been up to. Give them time. Ask them what they've been up to, and how they are. Take the initiative with them. You'll find that they'll be a lot more reasonable with the rules if they can see that you are being responsible. It may even help you to see why they make up such stupid rules in the first place!

Buy your Mum some flowers, and not just in March (that's when Mothering Sunday is...). Save up and take them out for a meal (not to Macdonalds). Actually, Anna and I took her Dad to Macdonalds, and he asked for the cutlery!

Go on, love them. They deserve it.

No questions asked?

But what if they demand that you do something which is un-Christian, or even anti-Christian?

Well it depends on what it is. If your Mum tells you to stop reading your Bible and do your homework, don't go all holy on her. Do what you are told. There are plenty of other times when you could read your Bible.

If you're told not to go to church, that may be a different story. Of course it may be a one-off, but if it's a blanket command, 'I'm telling you, no daughter of mine is ever going to be seen dead in that church', you may have to consider disobeying them in order to obey God.

And if one of your parents or a relation tries some form

of physical or sexual abuse, God certainly doesn't expect you to agree to that.

There may be some times when you have to disobey your parents in order to obey God. And these should be reluctant, prayerful, last-resort actions. But let's be clear—those times will be very rare, and for most of us, we won't be forced into that situation at all. And we should still try to honour our parents—keep up the communication.

Evangelising the olds?

Some people manage to help their parents become Christians. I know whole families who have become Christians through the witness of one teenager. But it's rare. For one thing, your parents have spent all your life telling you what to do and believe, and when the tables are turned, it's kind of tough on them. It takes astonishing humility for dear old Mum or Dad to do a turn around, and admit to you that you are right, and they are wrong.

Do explain your faith if they ask you to, but don't preach to them over the cornflakes. Gently probe to see if they are interested.

Focus your efforts on praying for them. It's the best thing you could do for them, after all.

Tidy your bedroom. That could be the only proof your Mum needs that something really significant has happened in your life.

Ask them to church. Not every Sunday, but now and then.

Love and obey them. They're very special people. Give them back a bit of love, even if it's costly.

Talk to them. Let them in on what you're thinking, and what you are doing.

DIGGING IN

1. Make a commitment to pray for your parents every day from now on.

2. Each day do something practical to help your parents. Don't wait to be asked, just get down and do something useful for them.

3. When you get in from school, sit down and tell your Mum or Dad what you have been doing. Make a commitment to spend, say, 15 minutes a day with them.

17

Hanging in there

...the best party ever

No one in the Bible ever said that being a Christian was going to be easy. It's not. Sometimes being a Christian is really tough. It's hard work. It takes up a lot of time. It can be a real struggle. Sometimes it's a grind. Sometimes it doesn't seem very rewarding.

Now and then you may wonder 'Is this really worth it?' Yes it is.

It's a bargain

Being a Christian is worth it because you get the best bargain the world has ever seen. You get your sins forgiven, and you get the gift of eternal life, all for free. That's not just a bargain, that's the most fantastic thing anyone has ever or will ever be offered. And it's all for free.

It's a relationship

Christianity is all about being loved by God. He's really nice and he loves you more than you can imagine. No matter what you go through, and no matter what other people may say, you can know for sure that you are friends with someone who knows you inside out, and no matter what you do, they'll still love you more than anyone else in the world.

It's exciting

Being a Christian is exciting because it is the only thing in the universe that can change you to become a different person. You can hang up your ideas about a career, a dog, a nice house, and holidays in the sun every summer. When you follow Jesus, all those sort of things somehow become less important, and there's no telling where you might end up! Being involved in something unique in the history of the universe has just got to be exciting.

It's worthwhile

Christianity is the only thing that will give you a real purpose in life, and a reason for living. And it's the only thing that really completely satisfies human beings. In fact, the Bible tells us that becoming a Christian makes you into a full human being. Sounds pretty worthwhile to me.

It's true

Lots of people are 'living a lie'. They are living in God's world, but are choosing to ignore him and all that he is wanting to give them. Being a Christian is wonderful, because it is true.

It's rewarding

Christianity is about being given eternal life by God. It's about going to Heaven. Of course there are benefits from being a Christian here and now. But the real reward is in Heaven. It will be the greatest reward anyone has ever had. And it's yours, waiting for you in Heaven.

Sometimes being a Christian will be easy. But often it won't be. And in the tough times, look ahead to the prize in Heaven. Eternal life, the best party ever.

And keep on hanging in there.